Hard

Yards

Throughout his long life, Bill Walker has always striven to be the best he can be at everything he has undertaken. What Bill has achieved required more than bundles of natural athletic ability and intelligence. It also required enormous amounts of determination, application, persistence and time. Bill wrote, "Without the hard work, the *Hard Yards*, I don't see my achievements in medicine, surgery, both in Australia and overseas, and my music, sports and Rotary would have been such a success."

Hard Yards

The Life and Times of a Third World Plastic Surgeon

William D. Walker
MB BS FRACS OAM

Lakehouse Publishing

Published by Lakehouse
Lake Macquarie City, NSW Australia

ISBN 9780648497660 Print Book
ISBN 9780648497653 eBook

NATIONAL
LIBRARY
OF AUSTRALIA

A catalogue record for this
book is available from the
National Library of Australia

Published in verdana with size 12 font.
Printed in Melbourne, Australia by Ingram Spark
(www.ingramspark.com).

DEDICATION

For my wife, Doris

CONTENTS

Illustrations

FOREWORD

My grandmother's house was in Maroubra Road, Pagewood. It had a huge mulberry tree in the backyard, a source of many stained fingers and clothes. In the side yard it had a bush nut tree, known, I discovered later, as a macadamia tree.

I had many cousins, uncles, and aunts and I remember an evening when everyone was gathered around my grandmother's grand piano in the front music room and a tall handsome young man and a young woman with a lot of reddish hair were seated side by side playing a furious duet. It was all impossibly exciting. This is my first memory of my Uncle Bill.

Over the years, he would drop in to visit his older brother, my father, often from somewhere exotic. Letters, postcards and photos would come from places you had never heard of.

My father was *always* tremendously proud of his young brother's achievements.

It has been a personal pleasure for me to assist Uncle Bill in writing his autobiography.

I would like to thank my friend, the author, Jan Mitchell, for her generous support and advice.

Bruce Walker,

Baulkham Hills 2020

INTRODUCTION

How often do we pass a person in the street and never have the privilege to know what contributions they have made in changing peoples' lives. Some call these people unsung heroes but I will call mine "Willy" who I have known for the past 45 years.

I first met Dr. William Walker in the operating theatres at Royal Newcastle Hospital in 1970. He was the first Plastic Reconstructive Surgeon in Newcastle and quite a novelty, very different from the regular prim and proper starchy surgeons. I had just registered as a nurse and found myself working as a scrub nurse in the operating theatre. He soon found an audience of nurses wanting to work with him listening to his jokes and stories and observing all his new surgical techniques as Newcastle was on a new wave of surgical procedures called Plastic/Reconstructive and Cosmetic Surgery.

Lake Macquarie Private Hospital was opened in 1973 as the first private hospital in Newcastle and was where I started in 1974 working as Willy's scrub nurse for the next 20 years. You certainly get to know a person very well in such a time span and we became friends as well as colleagues. The bulk of the procedures were facelifts, breast augmentations, tummy tucks and excision of skin cancers.

There wasn't a story or situation that Willy hadn't experienced or had done. He is the result of being the last born to a family of six sisters so he literally had seven mothers who constantly spoiled him. However, the saying goes "Behind every successful man there is a woman". This was Doris, whom he married after a five and a half months courtship and she absolutely idolised him.

Loving challenges and being competitive, Willy played many sports and musical instruments and swimming in the World Masters was a great achievement winning many gold medals. Being a bit eccentric one Christmas he brought his cello into the operating theatre to play carols.

My first of many volunteer missions away with Willy and Doris was to Uganda and Mozambique at the height of the AIDS epidemic. His attitude was that we were safe as long as we didn't have sex with the locals!

It was an experience to witness the generosity, care and kindness that these two people have for others in the developing world. Willy was a great teacher and was confronted with massive and horrific abnormalities. His treatment was always first world standard and he would never consider treatment that couldn't be followed up and completed by the local surgeon.

We travelled to many destinations: Papua New Guinea, Peru, Samoa, India, Philippines, Kiribati and many parts of China. The bulk of the operations were cleft lips and palates. I was always amazed at the stamina of Willy in his 80s standing bent over the tiny mouth of a small child operating for hours on end just to get through the huge volume of patients hoping for a life changing procedure.

I remember on a ward round post operation when he asked the interpreter to ask the mother if she was happy with the lip result. The mother looked up with a huge smile and tears in her eyes. Willy answered, "Paid in Full". Many of our missions have stories of sadness, poverty, diagnoses but unable to be treated and local corruption. Doris had a mastectomy and her bra where a prostheses was fitted was replaced with US dollars. These were handed out for food, transport and accommodation for the very poor.

On some missions, Doris was unable to come due to poor health. The volunteers on the team would ask if Willy and I were married. Willy would reply "Yes but not to each other, Thank God ".

Doris was the love of Willy's life and they had been through a lot. Imagine to have only two surviving children out of seven and still find fortitude to go and help the people of the developing countries free of charge!

After the passing of Doris in 2010, Willy was very lost and lonely but fortunately, he has found a new loving partner in Angela with whom he enjoys his twilight years swimming and socializing.

I have been very fortunate to have known William Downing Walker as colleague and very good friend. He has certainly used every opportunity to improve the lot of others and to give unconditionally through his Christian values.

Lyn Thorpe OAM
N.S.W. Senior Australian of the Year 2010

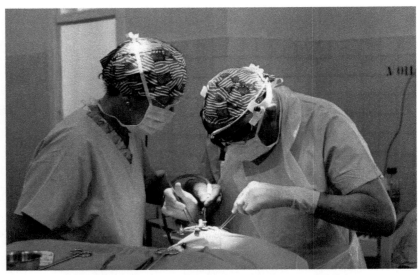

Willy and Lyn operating in Peru, 2004

1 EARLY DAYS

CHILDHOOD MEMORIES

We lived in a big house, where I was born, the youngest of eight surviving children. It had a slate tile roof and outside verandah on which I slept. We had a modest backyard with a large red-flowered flame tree. I used to climb to the top and give cheek to my mates who couldn't climb up as high as I could in my tree refuge. We made cubby houses in the backyard using any wood or cardboard we could find, held together with rope and wire ties. We played cowboys and Indians and made bows and arrows.

The family with two and a half year old Jim Chivas.
Earliest photo of Bill aged 6 years

My first memory is of being taken to the Sydney Harbour Bridge when it had just been opened in 1932. I tried to pick up a two-shilling coin but Mum unknowingly pulled me away.

My sister and I used to get up to mischief. Instigated by Olive, we would whistle taxis to stop and then hide behind the front fence. Olive would climb onto the roof and call out to passing friends then hide behind the lee of the roof leaving them wondering where she was.

I used to swing on a tree in the front yard jumping from one branch to another then fall to ground about nine feet below. One night at age nine years, I missed my branch and landed heavily on the ground below dislocating my left elbow. Friends took me to Eastern Suburbs Hospital as my parents had gone on business to the races. My arm was dislocated and I had the dislocation reduced under general anaesthetic. My parents arrived about 11pm.

"Would you like to stay overnight or go home now with your parents?"

"What's for breakfast?" was my reply, so important was food in those days of the depression.

On another occasion aged around five, I decided to run across the road to buy sweets. I counted three cars coming from the right and ran straight into the back wheel of a fourth car. I lay sprawled on the road.

The driver and others asked, "Where did the car hit you?"

"No, the car didn't hit me, I hit the car!" was my reply. There was no harm done.

Unfortunately, such was not the case for a three-year old a few doors away. He was playing in the gutter. A car driven by a learner driver (the pharmacist's fiancé with no licence and no permit) ran onto the child, mounting the kerb. The child's head was crushed under a back wheel and he later died in hospital. The driver's parents complained to Mum that it cost them sixty pounds for a barrister's fee to get an acquittal.

"You were lucky you didn't get a few years in gaol," said Mum.

We had several neighbours. The Crafts next door were true Cockneys from London having been born and lived within earshot of Bow Bells (The bells of St Mary Le Bow in Cheapside). Across the back lane lived the Bridges with two sons, Alan, (my age) and the younger Patrick as well as twin daughters. Their father was a bank manager. The children went to private schools so we didn't see as much of them but played together out of school time. Unfortunately, their father died in the surf, drowning following a heart attack. Alan became an Ear, Nose and Throat (ENT) Specialist practising in Canberra, and Patrick a prominent ENT Sydney Specialist with expertise in head and neck cancer particularly involving the base of the skull.

A few doors down the road lived a mother with a sole boy child my age, who obviously sought attention by not eating his food. His mother used to get this depression-starved Billy (me) to come and eat the lot as an example, but to no avail.

Men came around selling clothes props to hold up your clothes lines for clothes drying. Bottle-ohs would call for empty beer bottles, which they collected, being worth about one penny each.

We played a dangerous game in the back lane, which involved riding by hanging on the back of the ice cart when it came by.

I had an Indian friend named Basil who lived across the lane at the back. His father, Dr.Singh, ran a quiet medical practice, which involved visits by female clients in expensive cars. We suspected he might have been an illegal abortionist.

The Singhs billeted a group of visiting wrestlers, the Shahs, during their wrestling exhibitions. At age twelve, another boy challenged me to wrestle him and I won, pinning him to the ground.

"He must have had lessons from the Shahs," they said but it was not so. I was just quick with good reflexes.

MY CHILDHOOD SEXUAL EXPERIENCES

At age seven, I came to realise that adults placed a good deal of importance on an activity that consisted of genital contact man to woman (colloquially called a "fuck"). I felt, as children we should explore this activity. I decided to enlist a five-year-old girl, Cindy, who lived close by with her grandparents. We took her to a nearby unused house and after pants down pressed genitals together, me first, two boys later.

"I don't like this. Take me home", said Cindy, which I did.

On arrival home her guardians asked, "Where have you been Cindy, and what have you been doing?"

"I've been down to the empty house with Billy Walker, *having a fuck*!"

"*No I didn't*!" said I and ran home as guilty as hell.

Of course the guardians would soon realise no physical harm was done.

I learned two things: First, don't try anything sexual until you have found out how to do it and, secondly, *women tell.*

Reggie Craft was aged fourteen and older than us by several years. He had a hard manual job with thick hard skin. He used to get us soft-handed boys to masturbate him and I learned what it was from him.

An eight or nine year old girl named Ann from down Frenchman's Road took a fancy to me aged seven and invited me to go with her to Clovelly pictures. We each had sixpence to spend, three pence in and three pence to buy a lolly or ice cream but not both. We sat dreamily together during the show.

"Well, did you like that?" said Ann. "Would you like to come again?"

"No," said I and there ended our relationship. She later became a model.

Olive and I used to climb a large tree in a nearby park and wait quietly. We enjoyed watching American sailors having sex with their partners there.

OLIVE'S LEAVING HOME

Olive was a rebellious child and at age twelve, she decided to leave home after an argument with Mother. I was co-opted and we walked to Clovelly theatre and watched the men putting up large billposters of coming attractions. About nine pm Ollie decided we had nowhere to sleep except home. Olive received a good belting from Mum, I was allowed off. Never again did Olive leave home.

MISCHIEVOUS OLIVE

My father had a large Studebaker car with running boards on the outside and we used to go in it to Katoomba for day trips on a Sunday.

The car was kept parked in a carport at the back of the yard and there was an upwards slope to the back lane exit. Olive found out that if you put the car in reverse gear, took off the brake and turned the key to the starter motor, the car would leap backwards; take it out of gear and it would roll back to its original position. Repeating this was like being on a fun machine at a fair. The battery inevitably ran flat and Dad had to have it charged. He took away the keys and chastened Olive but there was no hiding as she was Dad's favourite.

I loved going to school and was a good student. I was not the dux of the class but usually finished in the upper third of the class in exams.

For a summer sport, we had a rather unfortunate introduction to cricket. All ages were put in each of four "houses" such that with no teaching as a twelve-year-old at the wicket I faced the school's fastest bowler aged sixteen and attempted to protect myself until he bowled me out soon after. When my team was in defence, my station was in the outfield in the hot sun. The team expected me to throw the ball back when it came my way. It was a most unhappy introduction to cricket and. I chose swimming instead. My parents somewhat wisely forbade me to play rugby league football, as it was too rough, they said. I now agree. I took up hockey instead and captained the school team in my last few years.

MEMORIES OF THE DEPRESSION

As a young four or five year old, I would go out and collect the milk which had been poured out into a large can hung on a nail on the side fence. We had four pints delivered daily. One day, on lifting the can up high from the nail in the fence, the can caught on something and spilled three quarters of its contents on the ground. I brought the remainder into Mum and gave me a rare beating, which I never forgot.

"We will have to make it do for the rest of the day," said Mum as we had no money for extra milk. Mum duly suspended me from my milk-collecting job.

I was born five months before the infamous Wall Street crash of October 1929. I remember food was always short so we bought the cheapest meat and 'tripe' was a regular offering. We used dripping instead of butter and bought cheap broken biscuits from the grocer.

One time in fourth class, my mother asked me if the teacher caned me in class. "Oh yes, about once a day."

Mum fronted up to the classroom and accosted the teacher, who denied the frequency of caning. He punished me because I talked too much in class to my next seated partner.

"Why don't you just separate them?" asked Mum. The teacher did so and it solved the problem of talking and caning.

My older working-age sisters had to walk six miles to collect the dole. I remember seeing streets full of 'For Sale' notices on repossessed housing. The bailiffs would come and take your furniture when you couldn't pay the rent. We mended our own clothes and our shoes with "chrome hide" and glue on synthetic rubber soles. We had practically no toys but I remember each one I did have. I had a dinky car at age three which I loved but sadly grew too large for it.

Aged five, I started at Randwick Primary School. Later in first year high school at Randwick we had a teacher named Mr. Smart who was a sadistic disciplinarian. We were learning algebra and he would put a problem up on the board and ask us to solve it. If you got it wrong, the teacher hit us with the sharp edge of a ruler across the back of our fingers. If he caught you correcting your answer you got an extra whack. Virtually the whole class received several of these punishments every day. Parents noticed the marks on our fingers and reported to the headmaster. Mr. Smart (we called him "smart by name and smart by nature") was transferred out of the school and given a posting to somewhere in far Western New South Wales - out the 'back of Bourke'.

I swam in races in my first year at Randwick High School but can't recall having any great success but think I came third in a breaststroke final.

In mid-year 1941, we moved from our Randwick house to Katoomba. My mother and father always liked the Blue Mountains and we often took a day trip by car to the resort. Mother inherited some money from relatives in the UK and she bought three houses in Katoomba with it. The family moved into one some eight months before the Japanese midget submarine attack in Sydney. This resulted in an exodus of some 80,000 Sydney residents to the Blue Mountains. My sisters Olive and June trained in nursing and graduated at the Blue Mountains District Hospital.

In my second year at Katoomba High School, I won seven races at Blackheath Swimming Pool. I was totally untrained. I realise that I must have been a naturally good swimmer. I used to win my age races every two years when in the oldest age of the two-year range. In my final year of high school, I won a fifty-yard breaststroke race in a record time of forty-two seconds. That record stood for over ten years.

On one occasion aged about fourteen, I was practising tennis, hitting a ball against the front wall of the house. Olive came out screaming, "Can't you stop that, I am trying to sleep?"

She had been on night duty.

"No." I replied whereupon she hit me in the chest as hard as she could.

Olive said later that she realised at that point she could no longer physically dominate me as she had in the past.

At home, we used a wood-fired stove and oven for cooking and it was my job to cut the wood. I had a friend called "Jeeps" Henderson, an orphan who lived with an ageing Scottish aunt. We taught ourselves how to cut down dead trees and saw them up for fuel. With no mechanical chain saws, we did it all by hand with saws, axes and wedges. We became expert in the use of saw and axe. We hiked the trails around Katoomba and tested our strength in walking up the Giant Stairway of some 800 steps at Echo point, not stopping for a rest.

When I was twelve, Dad bought Olive and me a secondhand bicycle each. These had no gears and so we walked up the steepest hills. We were riding down towards Katoomba Falls when some gravel caused me to come off my bicycle. I fractured my left wrist and had it set by Dr Alcorn at Katoomba Hospital. I learned to go a little slower downhill.

My mother and father went to Sydney on Thursdays to run Dad's business as a bookmaker at the races, returning on Sunday. I looked after myself for three days each week, cooking all my own meals.

My sister June, having had a broken romance in Sydney, fell in love with one Bert Falconer who was a manager of NORCO Dairy products. He used to boast that he could get us any amount of butter coupons. Butter was rationed and in short supply. Bert was a divorcee and my father disliked him, which only served to make June more ardent and rebellious.

Dad felt that from the way Bert was throwing money around, he must be embezzling it from NORCO. He suggested to their management that an urgent audit was required. There was a deficiency of some two thousand pounds. The company was all set to have Bert fined or gaoled when Bert's father (who was well up in the Masonic Lodge) put up the missing money and the case was dropped. Bert later became a car mechanic working for a transmission gear company as well as running a private backyard car-repair business. June and Bert married in about 1946. They had one son who they named "Bill" after me.

I sat for my Leaving Certificate in 1945 aged sixteen and passed five subjects with 'Bs", but unfortunately failed in English which was a prerequisite for any University course. My teachers at Katoomba High School wisely advised me to repeat the final fifth year. This I did achieving a pass with two As and four Bs. I liked French and sat the honours paper but with no extra teaching failed to get the honours.

My parents christened me 'Billy', which was my father's nickname on the racecourse.

I had been told, "That's a girl's name" so for many years I disliked my christened name.

A sibling was named William but he had died before I was born. At the Leaving Certificate presentation the Lord Mayor called the head teacher over asking, "Isn't this a mistake, shouldn't this be William not Billy?"

"No, that's his name." she said.

I decided to change it to William by Deed Poll when I was twenty-one, the eligible age to do so, which I did. I have been called Billy, Bill, William, Willy and recently, *Will* (the Royals!). My closest friends call me Bill and I reserve 'William' for cheques and important documents.

2 MY HERITAGE

I first saw daylight on 14th May 1929 in our house at 64 Frenchman's Road, Randwick, not far from the Randwick Racecourse where my father worked as a bookmaker. I was the 11th child of my parents.

My father was firstly a grocer and my mother came from a wealthy Victorian family who considered William Walker was too low class to marry their daughter, Alice Elizabeth Lawrence Williams. The Williams were successful engineers.

Alice never went out to work and learned the piano for ten years in Birmingham from a good teacher, a Mrs. Knox. She achieved her Licentiate of the Royal College of Music (LRCM), its highest award, and usually the last exam before launching a career as a performing soloist musician. It is also a music teaching qualification so Mother taught ten pupils for something to do.

Her parents had selected an Earl for her to marry but Mother found him completely unattractive calling him a "chinless wonder". Her parents refused to allow her to marry her choice, <u>William Edward Howarth Walker </u>(born 3rd March 1882 in Salford, Manchester). Both Mum and Dad were raised as strict Anglicans attending church three times a week.

At eighteen, Mother became pregnant but was still denied marriage. The baby died at birth and she was told, "Serves you right for disobeying your elders". This was not practising Christian compassion but rather class distinction and led to both my parents discarding their Anglican faith. The baby was called William.

Mother married Dad in 1908, aged twenty-two, and above the legal age of twenty-one when you could marry without parental consent.

The Williams family found Dad a job as a steward on board the Cunard Line hoping the long absences at sea would break up Mum's relationship with him. Dad did several overseas trips to Argentina and other places and finally after a voyage to Australia, decided to emigrate with family and two children Edward (Ted) and Edith (Edie) in 1912.

THE WALKER NAME

As far as we can discover, Dad's family were Scottish Walkers several generations back. In England, my father worked as a stage magician for about three years until the business folded due to not performing enough new tricks. He used to do party tricks involving putting six pennies in a matchbox. He would make them all disappear, showing us the signed empty matchbox only for them to reappear in the box later. I asked Dad to teach me the trick but he said magicians were not allowed to divulge their secrets otherwise this trick would become useless. I think I inherited some of his dexterous hand skills that were useful to me as a surgeon.

Dad's first job in Sydney was as a window cleaner. He later ran a convenience store with pool tables for soldiers from Singleton Army Camp. Post World War 1, he took up bookmaking at Randwick Racecourse but lost out early until he learnt the tricks of the trade. He had a rails stand at Randwick which he sold, much to his financial disadvantage as those that didn't sell all became wealthy. In bookmaking, Dad worked the "ponies" which were thoroughbred horses of less than 14.2 hands, ridden by jockeys at one of four dedicated pony courses (Kensington, Rosebery, Victoria Park and Ascot) between Sydney City and Botany. After a period of success, the Ponies folded during the depression years of the 1930s. Dad did country race meetings but mainly greyhounds and trotters. We children had to write up the dog form so that Dad could produce a Market Sheet (used for tipping), most essential for bookmakers. He taught me how to clerk for country meetings as his assistant. His pricing business continued until his death in 1948.

Dad developed Type II diabetes at fifty-five and died from pneumonia as a complication of a Bells Mania aged sixty-six. His son-in-law, George Yendall, with Mother as administrator, continued the pricing business well into the 1960s, producing tipping sheets that concentrated on greyhounds and used the methods laid down by Dad.

My mother, <u>Alice Elizabeth Lawrence Williams,</u> (opposite) was born 26th April 1886 at Kinver near Stourbridge in the Midlands of England and died 28th April 1973 aged eighty-seven. The Lawrence part of the name is said, in family legend, to have come from a French nobleman who escaped the French Revolution by rowing a boat across the English Channel with his wife and seven children aboard. Mother said she had a child every two years after breast-feeding contraception cut out. Mother had excessive bleeding with her two deliveries before me, due to adherent placenta that required manual removal. Her GP-obstetrician told her that a further pregnancy was too dangerous and that he would abort one. She had no period for several months at age 45 and thought she had reached the change of life. Whilst playing cards one night she felt a kick in the abdomen and a subsequent examination by her GP revealed an advanced pregnancy of four and a half months. "It is too late to abort," said her GP and the result was that I was born.

It was Mother's Day 14th May 1929 and after six daughters, Mum said it was the best ever Mother's Day present.

THE WILLIAMS NAME

My Mother told us the Williams forebears were skilled engineers. She recalls her great grandfather, James Williams, was an engineer employed by Tanges Engineering Company of Birmingham (originally of Cornwall) who were asked to help in the launching of The Great Eastern liner by I.K.Brunel. Tanges specialised in hydraulic equipment and held the first patents for the hydraulic jack.

Alice Elizabeth Lawrence Williams

They also built steam engines and much later diesel engines. The Great Eastern was the largest ship ever built at the time and unsurpassed in size for another forty years. The vessel was too heavy to be launched in the conventional manner. Grandfather Williams designed and built a series of hydraulic rams which, on the second attempt, successfully launched the Great Eastern. It was the 31st January, 1858.

Another Williams built a working model of a tin mine in Cornwall, which was later placed in a museum.

My mother's grandfather, <u>Samuel James Downing,</u> was born on 8th March 1832 and died in 1900 aged sixty-eight.

THE ORIGIN OF THE NAME DOWNING.

In 1680, Baronet Sir George Downing was a man of considerable wealth who built a number of houses in London. Many buildings and streets were named after him including the street of the Prime Minister's residence, 10 Downing Street. He was also responsible for the acquisition of New York from the Dutch and there are more streets named after him there.

Sir George Downing's descendant, Samuel James Downing, was one of four sons who all started their working lives as iron mill labourers. Samuel was a mill furnace-man, a heavy, hot job at the bottom of the labouring job scale. He saved up enough money by age twenty-four to buy a block of land on which he built a hotel named The Yew Tree Inn in Albion Road, West Bromwich. It had been named after a large yew tree facing the front, which had long since gone when the pub was built. The hotel was close to eight factories and so had a healthy patronage of thirsty workers. The Yew Tree Inn made a fortune for Samuel and by age thirty he built an ironworks with three associates. His ironworks had considerable financial success, making gun carriers for the Franco-Prussian War of 1870-71. He later bought out his partners and was sole owner of Richmond Ironworks when he died. He was a magistrate and Justice of the Peace and once sat for a seat on the town council but lost to another candidate. He did not contest the seat again.

My mother had great admiration for her grandfather saying he was a 'lucky self-made man'. He built a large house called *The Norlands* in Erdington. It had twelve bedrooms and twelve housemaids. My mother was intrigued by the twelve bells which, when rung summoned a particular housemaid. She loved visiting there. The house was sufficiently large to be used as a rehab hospital for injured and recovering World War II soldiers.

The Downing name was given to many of Samuel's descendants as in my case. I also gave my two sons the name and likewise my nephew, sister Olive's son, John Downing Sekoranja. Recently my great grandson received the name Theodore Downing Walker, continuing the family tradition.

MY SIBLINGS

The siblings: Bill, Olive, June, Joyce, Lawrie, Bessie, Edie, and Ted. Photo: 1996

William - stillborn? 1904.

<u>Edward Howarth Walker</u> (Ted) was born 9th September 1909 and died September 1995 aged eighty-six.

My Brother Ted was five months short of twenty years older than me and had left home before I knew him. Ted learned the baking trade and made bread in Sydney near Kensington. A large company tried to buy him out but Ted refused to sell saying he made better bread, which was probably right. They ran him out of business by cutting off his flour supply. Ted hated the capitalist system and joined the Communist Party. At the age of fourteen, I probably knew more about Karl Marx than about Jesus Christ. Ted was a miner and later became a fitter and turner through a hands-on apprenticeship and worked for Australian Paper Manufacturers until retirement at age sixty-five.

Ted's cars never saw a garage as he did all his own repairs. He taught me how to disassemble my Wolseley car engine and have it reconditioned and later the front wheel kingpins so I had a good basic knowledge of car mechanics. In Manchester, years later I re-conditioned my Rover 90 gearbox whilst living at Baguley Hospital doctors' quarters, after which I became the medical staffs' car advisory person.

Ted married Doreen Hill in 1940 and had two sons, Edward, who became a General Practitioner at Balmain and Bruce, who worked as a high school teacher and school counsellor.

Curiously, Ted was a Mason and non-religious although Masons are required to believe in God.

Edith Lavinia Flecknoe (Edie) was born 29th March 1911 and died February 2005 aged ninety-four years.

Sister Edie became a seamstress or tailor and made clothes to order until she married Doug Flecknoe. Both my brother Ted and his friend

Doug Flecknoe were inventive, talented and clever men whose opportunities were lost through the Great Depression. Edie was also an accomplished pianist. She had two children, Jocelyn (Joy), who although she completed a degree in Earth Sciences, spent her working life in secretarial and office management positions, and Don who became an architect. Doug Flecknoe, in World War II built a floating torpedo bomb, which he offered to the Navy. It was not accepted as it was less efficient than what was already available.

Bessie Rosalind Chivas (Bess) was born 30th January 1915 and died on 29th December 2009 aged ninety-four years. Bess was my godmother at Baptism. She worked as a housemaid and, at age eighteen, met James Chivas (Jim), a carpenter. They married soon afterwards and their first child, James (also Jim), was born. He was my parents' first grandchild and I was only four and a half years senior to my nephew.

Jim trained at the Conservatorium principally in violin and became a secondary school music teacher. He switched to Primary Teaching and later became a lecturer in teacher education, having completed a research Master's Degree in Education. Early retirement produced another change of direction when Jim took up employment with the Rural Fire Service, later working in a consultancy role.

Bess's second child, June, trained as a Pharmacist and she worked in both the UK and Australia. Their third child, Anne, trained in both singing and piano. She sang with the Philharmonic Choir and worked for the BBC in the UK, which led to work with the ABC in Sydney as a program producer. After the children were off her hands, Bess entered Psychiatric Nursing eventually becoming the Sister-in-Charge of the first Children's' Psychiatric Ward at North Ryde Mental Hospital.

Samuel Walker was born in 1917 and died eight months later from tubercular meningitis.

Lawrence Yendall (Lawrie) was born on 12th November 1920 and died January 2010.

Lawrie was a talented and successful prize-winning cake maker and decorator, who ran a wedding catering service. She became a Dietician at Royal North Shore Hospital until her retirement but continued to paint and decorate ceramics. She had a flair for design and came first in a chocolate making Technical College course later in her life. Her husband, George Yendall, was an inspector for Sydney trams and later ran my father's race-pricing business. He died relatively young in his fifties. They had two daughters, Lorraine who became a geologist and librarian, and Rosalie who became a nursing sister. Lorraine and Rosalie each had three daughters, one of whom, Lorraine's daughter Georgette, became a General

Practitioner and another daughter, Jennifer, an Aged Care Worker.

Mary was stillborn (1921).

Joyce Ester Howe was born on the 2nd July 1922 and died on the 8th May 2010.

Joyce was probably the most academically gifted of all the Walker children. She passed her Leaving Certificate with a Pass good enough to get a scholarship into any faculty of any University. She applied for Teachers College, easily qualifying for a scholarship but Dad insisted his children had to work and so she became a secretary. Joyce married Doug Howe, an engineer with the Maritime Services Board and they had two children, Ronald and Janet.

In her 40s, Joyce applied for and was granted a teachers college scholarship and passed all her exams with flying colours. She followed this with a Master's Degree and became a school counsellor, later becoming a supervisor in the Education Department School Counselling Service. Joyce developed severe asthma and was on steroids until she died aged eighty-eight. Her son Ronald became an Electrical Engineer and completed a PhD. His sister Janet completed an Arts Degree and Teaching Diploma but later ran a successful health food stores business.

June Patricia Falconer was born on 17th March 1924 and died on 29th December 2013.

June was a highly intelligent woman and in her youth was always fighting with Joyce mostly over who would do the household chores. After leaving school, she took a job as a process worker with S.T. Leigh cigarette paper manufacturers, packing cigarette papers. When she was eighteen, June fell in love with a Catholic boy named Vince from a strong Catholic family. His family would have nothing to do with Anglicans even though June was not religious and from a non-practising Anglican family. She was out of bounds for their son and they made sure the relationship was broken up.

After June broke her leg in an accident, the family GP, Dr. Allcorn, suggested to Dad that both June and Olive would be suited to nursing. We moved to Katoomba in 1941 and June did her nursing qualification at the Blue Mountains District Hospital in Katoomba. June went on to Crown Street Women's' Hospital for her obstetric training and later did her Respiratory Diseases training at Randwick Chest hospital (The Prince of Wales Hospital) where she was Night Superintendent (Matron) for twenty-four years until her retirement.

With her husband, Bert Falconer, she had one son, William, who worked in Real Estate. June moved to a hobby farm at Tewantin near Noosa in Queensland and, after Bert died, married Norm Duckworth. Norm developed dementia and died in a nursing home.

<u>Olive Maud Sekoranja</u> was born on the 9th March 1927.

Olive, my nearest sister, was a great playmate of mine in childhood, as recorded elsewhere in this narrative ("Mischievous Olive"). She was headstrong and persuaded our mother not to have her return to school after a bout of scarlet fever before Christmas.

Olive and Bill Circa 2012

She turned fourteen early the next year and was not pursued by the authorities This was *before* she had completed her Intermediate Certificate, a most basic requirement for many jobs. She followed June into a packing job at S.T. Leigh and, like sister June, Olive was far too intelligent for this type of work.

She started on her nursing career when we moved to Katoomba. To do this required her to study and pass a nurses' entrance exam at which, not unexpectedly, she did brilliantly. She similarly sailed through her nursing training. She did maternity nursing at Crown Street Women's' Hospital followed by Tresillian training (baby care) afterwards.

Olive obtained a job in Obstetrics at Griffith District Hospital in the Riverina area of NSW. There she met John Sekoranja who was working as a wards man at the hospital. John was a happy, intelligent Displaced Person from Slovenia (Yugoslavia) who had been put into forced labour in the boot making trade in Germany during the War. He escaped from Communist Yugoslavia into Greece and spent time in camps in Italy before being accepted by the Australian Government as a refugee. This was followed by the inevitable stint on the Snowy Mountains Scheme.

John and Olive married in 1953. He was a skilled shoe repairer and bootmaker and, together with Olive doing shoe sales, had very successful businesses in Cooma and Canberra.

John could speak eight languages. He and I had a great relationship. Olive and John had three children: Rosemary, who completed a degree in

Business Management and works in the Commonwealth Public Service in Canberra; Rhonda, who completed a degree in Librarianship and Information Services and, like Rosemary, works in the Commonwealth Public Service; and John, who worked for quite a few years in Information Technology for a US Multinational, but with a change of career, has recently bought a vineyard and trained as a vintner.

3 FINDING A CAREER

When I had passed the Leaving Certificate, I had the enormous decision as to what profession to enter. I fancied Engineering and did not want to be a burden financially on my parents so applied for fifteen jobs as an apprentice towards a trade certificate. As I had only two B passes in LC mathematics, they overlooked me. My last maths teacher wasn't helpful in getting me good passes.

My sisters June and Olive were keen for me to do medicine, as were my parents, who held our local General Practitioner in high esteem. It was Open University and you could pay your own way as long as you had matriculated. It seemed like a good idea at the time.

In 1947, a large number of ex-servicemen who, on discharge from the forces, were allowed to complete a Leaving Certificate, pass and without selection, were able to choose any university course they liked even with only a basic five B Leaving Certificate pass. Consequently, we had over 600 entrants into medicine in my first year at Sydney University and ex-service personnel accounted for at least one third of those. Students were allowed three failures and three repeated years on their way to graduation. A number became virtually perpetual university students, never graduating.

Studying second year medicine

My parents billeted me with my sister Joyce and her husband, Doug Howe, at their flat at Maroubra Beach. Doug was an engineer with the Maritime Services Board and they had two children, Ronald, not yet at school, and new-born baby Janet. Doug helped me with my first year studies and as a result, I obtained credit passes in Physics and Chemistry.

Doug taught me to play chess. His friend Bernard Mills was a chess genius who could play eight chess games against eight opponents simultaneously and beat them all. He analysed our games and showed us where we had missed obvious checkmate opportunities.

Bernard Mills was a Professor of Radio Physics and designed the *Mills Cross Radio Telescope* built near Parkes NSW. Bernard spent a lot of time analysing radio waves from outer space. He once said to me that he wished he could have done something useful for society as I was going to do in medicine. Bernard's wife was a Russian emigrant and highly intelligent. She topped the Leaving Certificate in her final year at school and entered medicine at Sydney University. She excelled in the non-clinical bio-medical science years, but in the last three clinical years of the medicine course, where you had to examine patients to make a diagnosis, she failed miserably. After failing her final year three times, she gave up.

I enjoyed my first year at Sydney University. We had a Zoology Professor who arrived at 9:05 am for his 9 am lecture and had the lecture room doors locked so that latecomers could not come in. A salutary disciplinary act.

As part of zoology, we had the opportunity to dissect a stingray at home in the bath and learn the basic anatomy of living organisms. I enjoyed that. I passed first year medicine with two credits.

My father became ill in 1948 with an acute mania known as "Bell's Mania" in which the patient is hypermanic and never goes to sleep. After a week they are exhausted and die. Dad had had Type II Diabetes from age fifty-five. They put him in a padded cell at Callan Park Hospital and gave him injections of paraldehyde to quieten him down. He developed pneumonia and died in a week at age sixty-six in mid-1948.

I applied for and was granted a university bursary scholarship as an impecunious student with a good record having passed first and second year when the failure rate was 50% for the first exam and about 50% for the post (deferred second go) exam. Many of the ex-forces personnel failed. After my father died, I became Mum's keeper driving the car to University and her to the races on Saturday nights.

There was a sixteen year-old girl living a few doors away with whom there was a mutual attraction. She was from a Catholic family and even though my mother was a lapsed Anglican, she still had the age-old anti-Catholic ideology. One Saturday night, my friend "Mary" called at our house, knocking on the door. I was studying in my room. Mum answered the door.

"I would like to see Bill and talk to him," said Mary.

"Sorry, no. You can't see him. He is studying for University and can't be disturbed. He will be studying for the next six years!" said Mother.

I was shocked to hear all this. I realised that Mum was bound to interfere with any romantic relationship she hadn't approved of. No one short of a princess or heiress would be good enough for her precious Billy. Once, she did arrange a meeting with a bookmaker's daughter (a wealthy family) but I found the girl most unattractive. My sister Olive also arranged a blind date for me with one of the hospital nurses but again there was no attraction.

My brother Ted obviously had similar problems with Mother. He used to take a bottle of wine and a blanket in the car when he went off to meet Doreen, his girlfriend. They broke off their relationship only to find each other still single six years later. Ted was thirty-one.

Mum said to Ted, "What's going on between you and Doreen?"

"Well, you might as well know now, because you'll eventually find out. We were married a month ago." replied Ted.

After they married, Doreen returned to live with her parents and Ted went back to Captains Flat where he worked as a miner. Doreen didn't tell her parents either for some months. Eventually they moved in together and had two sons, Edward (Eddie) and Bruce.

Third year medicine was only two terms long, finishing off the basic science course. I had trouble concentrating and studying, possibly related to Dad's death, and I failed all three subjects, anatomy, physiology and biochemistry. I was not granted a post exam and so had to repeat the year. This left me with no occupation for the last three months of the year so I took a labouring job at the Holden Factory across the road from the house in Pagewood, where we had moved from Katoomba. The factory made refrigerators and I was given a job as a "fixer" sorting out problems with machines that weren't working correctly. It was a useful time.

One of my first jobs was labouring on the construction of a swimming pool. The first day we shovelled mud out of the pool into wheelbarrows, all day for eight hours. It nearly killed me and, with aching back and arms, I went home and slept for twelve hours.

Doug Howe got me a job on the dock works in Sydney as a machine minder for two conveyors loading wheat. One ring, start the machines; two rings, stop the machines. It was a most boring job but paid well.

"What happens if I get it wrong and start a machine inadvertently?"

"Someone did that once and caught a worker on the conveyor belt breaking both his legs!"

"Now you tell me!"

My brother, Ted, worked as a maintenance fitter and turner at Australian Paper Manufacturers in Botany. At Christmas each year the plant closed down for a month and all the pipes carrying seawater to the power station had to be cleared of seaweed and mussels which grew in the inside to a depth of about four inches. After a few days in the hot Australian summer, the shells would rot and create a powerful stench. We had to get in the three-foot diameter pipe and scrape off the sea growth with shovels. We had a light on a long lead for vision. For ventilation, I devised large sheets of cardboard, which fitted in the manholes and faced towards the breeze. This provided ventilation without which you couldn't have worked for more than five or ten minutes before needing a break. We could extend our working time to fifteen to twenty minutes before emerging for fresh air. We were paid well at about one and a half to two times the normal rate, for danger money and weekend work.

The outside three-foot pipe was about four hundred metres long. There was also a two-foot diameter pipe into the power plant and you could only crawl on your elbows and toes one-way in and the same way out. It was quite claustrophobic.

Ted did a job machining grooves into large stainless steel plates for use in a paper pulp refiner, grinding the pulp to a much finer degree. If you made an error of one thousandth of an inch in one fin, you had to start again to get it right, every fin the same. It took the average machinist seven to eight days to complete the job. Ted worked out a way to get it down to seven hours. As a result, he was asked to extend his retirement from sixty-five to seventy years of age. He refused.

I passed my third year of medicine on the second go and received a placement at Royal Prince Alfred Hospital for my clinical years. I found no trouble taking histories and examining patients. I had good hands and good diagnostic skills.

I was allocated to the Women's Hospital at Paddington for my three months obstetrics training. I quite liked obstetrics and read Grantly Dick Reid's book on painless childbirth in which he teaches meditation, relaxation and to let it all happen naturally. I achieved much success going around the labour ward and practicing his methods on patients who were slow or doing poorly. My fellow students called me 'Grantly Dick Willy'. I decided to be an obstetrician but when jobs came around at the end of the year, all the higher academically qualified doctors got the jobs not an 'also ran' like me. With the litigation that has followed, I am glad I missed out.

Olive was doing her obstetric training at Crown Street Women's' Hospital, a two-year course, while I was in fourth year medicine. She brought home to our Pagewood residence a friend named Bonnie Kelly, who was also doing her obstetric training. Bonnie took an instant liking to me and we went swimming together. Before long, we were in bed making love, with me losing my virginity at twenty-one. We took advantage of

Mum's absences to use my bedroom. I also had the Wolseley car and I would drive at night to a quiet spot on the golf course. On one occasion we were interrupted by a policeman who moved us on.

Bonnie took me home to meet her mother who lived in a rented house in St Ives, a northern Sydney suburb. I got the impression that I wasn't classy enough for her daughter. Coming from the lower class Randwick area was not up to standard. I had noticed that at University parties, the girls from the Upper North Shore quickly lost interest in you if you came from lower class areas such as Randwick or Pagewood.

Bonnie was two years older than me and was interested in marriage and children, whereas I had no plans to marry until after graduation. After four or five months, we split up and Bonnie took up an obstetrics job on Norfolk Island. She married a Quintal, who was a Bounty descendant and had three children, remaining on Norfolk Island for the rest of her life. She took up flying light aircraft as I did later in life and surprisingly enough we both trained at Cessnock Flying School although at different times.

I was on a flying holiday with the Flying Rotarians to the USA and Alaska when we visited a town called Norfolk in the USA. One of the Flying Rotarians mentioned her acquaintance with Bonnie Quintal from Norfolk Island.

"Of course, you wouldn't know her, would you?"

"Know her? Yes, she took my virginity!"

My clinical years passed quickly without problems, as I was always comfortable examining patients and making diagnoses.

I passed my M.B., B.S (Bachelor of Medicine, Bachelor of Surgery) in the 1953 finals and received my Degree in January 1954. There was a list of all the Hospital jobs available and you selected your choice numbered from one on to the end of the list. Newcastle Hospital was the only one that guaranteed a second or third years training and was my Number 1 choice. All the teaching hospitals were highly sought after but only gave one year of training, with a one in three chance of a second year.

I was allocated to Cessnock Hospital in the Hunter Valley, a hospital of 140 beds. I had a co-resident in Dr. Paul Shagrin and we did a one in two on call.

On my first day, the Superintendent showed me over the hospital and at the end of the corridor, I saw Sister Doris Hyams with the Matron. Doris claims she took one look at me and said to herself, "I am going to marry him", which she later did!

At the end of each night's work, you would meet the night sister and discuss any patients that might need attention during the night. Somehow,

Doris would always be there and chat me up. She found out I liked western movies and invited me to see "Shane" with Alan Ladd.

"Oh, I've seen that film." I said.

"Why not come and see it again with me," said Doris. I did and realised she had designs on me from that day on.

Doris Hyams, aged 20 (circa 1952)

Just Married 24th January 1954

Doris took me to her Christadelphian Church meeting in a tiny church building in Cessnock, with about a dozen members. I thought they were a harmless lot but not my style.

After a whirlwind courtship, Doris and I decided to get married. Doris' religious beliefs demanded that she remain a virgin until after marriage so I decided we would have no engagement and get married in two weeks.

As Christadelphians don't marry outside their religious group, we had a Registry Office wedding in Cessnock with five witnesses, my sister Bessie, my mother, Doris' parents and a friend. I had asked all the family to come but, as most of them were anti-Doris, none came to the wedding. Two of my sisters had taken Doris aside and told her to push off and forget me.

We had a wedding reception in Doris' house with a chicken meal and about eighteen to twenty guests. We lived in the Cessnock Hospital residents' quarters with Dr Shagrin in a four-bedroom house.

My first year as a resident doctor at Cessnock was a great learning experience. I was designated anaesthetist and gave over 1000 anaesthetics in my first year. I became skilled at intubation, which proved useful later in my career.

At Cessnock, all General Practitioners practised surgery and I saw some of the worst surgery ever, such that I decided that I could only do better. One failed diagnosis of appendicitis in an over-sixty-year old resulted in his death. Cases that were doing poorly were referred to specialists at Newcastle.

My co-house officer, Dr. Paul Shagrin, seemed to have an obsessive-compulsive mental illness and was forever taking notes and checking up on things. He later had a modified partial frontal lobotomy in the USA, which did him no good. Even later, he had a partial thalamotomy (destruction of a small part of the thalamus in the brain) an almost experimental operation, which made him worse. He married and then suicided two years later, not able to cope with life.

Dr. Chambers and Dr. Moffat invited me to be an assistant in practice at Cessnock's largest general practice. It was a busy practice with a one in three roster. At 6 pm at the end of the day's consulting, I would still have to do eleven or twelve house calls. These were divided into two and, if on call, any extras added on to your night's work, which might not finish until 1 am. If you were the second on call, your five or six house calls would keep you up until 10 or 11 pm. It was a very heavy load of work. I found general practice somewhat repetitive and boring. At the end of the year, I resigned. Dr. Moffat's wife had told Doris that she was not allowed to continue working as a nurse as it was too demeaning to the practice. What rubbish! It was also a loss of our income.

Dr. Chambers found me a senior house officer job at Parramatta Hospital in 1956. This was one of the best jobs with a lot of learning particularly in orthopaedics and general surgery.

I met up with Hayden Skinner, a co-senior house officer, who encouraged me to start studying for the primary Fellow of the Royal College of Surgeons (FRCS). This I did. We also did obstetrics at Parramatta and, on one occasion, the rain caused the Nepean River to flood, such that a patient having her eighth child could not get to Windsor Hospital and her G.P. obstetrician. Labour became obstructed and a most skilful obstetrician, Dr. Small, had to do a very difficult forceps delivery of a big baby. After a twenty to thirty minutes struggle with Dr Small sweating, a live healthy baby and mother ensued.

"I hope I don't have to do another one like that," said Dr. Small.

I often wondered whether the flood had directed the patient to better treatment and outcome. Surely, God had a hand in this as he has used a flood before?

At Parramatta Hospital, I came to realise that my knowledge of paediatrics was deficient and so I applied for a job in paediatrics at the Princess Margaret Hospital for Children in Subiaco, Perth, Western Australia.

In January 1957, Doris and I drove our Humber Hawk car across the Nullabor Plains. There were over 1000 miles of dirt road with potholes twelve feet across carrying fine silt, which would penetrate doors and windows. You had to fill up at every bowser, as there were one hundred and eighty or more miles between petrol stations.

P.M.H. was my most enjoyable hospital job and I would have become a paediatric surgeon if the opportunity occurred which unfortunately it didn't.

MEMORIES OF PRINCESS MARGARET HOSPITAL

I spent the year 1957 as a junior resident at the Princess Margaret Hospital for Children and it proved to be the most enjoyable year of all my years of hospital training. The reason I went there was because I could not get a job in paediatrics in New South Wales as, at the change of the year, all the clever academic doctors got first choice.

Perth didn't have any medical graduates until I got there. They relied on NSW and SA doctors for the specialist jobs. Doris and I were accommodated in the hospital quarters.

The medical superintendent, Dr. Godfrey, ran the hospital with excellent efficiency. He held daily seminars, which all doctors were required to attend, to discuss the running of the hospital and sort out any problems. Breakfast was held in the doctors' dining room and I remember a kind, oldish lady who insisted we stay for a cooked breakfast of bacon, eggs and tomatoes, done to perfection.

The P.A. system was handled by a lovely lady who would call out your name and requirements twice indicating any degree of urgency. It was a very efficient system far better than the modern electronic devices.

There was a roster for us each in turn in the various wards. The gastro ward almost ensured you would get a bout of gastro enteritis (G.E.). The outpatients had a sister in charge monitoring all arrivals so that any seriously ill babies could receive urgent treatment. Some extreme cases of gastro enteritis died before treatment was started. We learned well how to manage G.E.

Similarly, we had an epidemic of meningococcal septicaemia while I was there, some children dying within hours of onset. I recall one small child dying within five hours of the onset of symptoms. I learned how to recognise the disease and septic rash, which later served me well in Queensland when I was faced with a solitary case of meningococcal septicaemia. Fortunately, in that case, I was able to save the patient.

We also had an epidemic of croup in winter, with children arriving in extreme anoxia from a blocked airway. My senior consultants were not very experienced at doing an emergency tracheostomy. I managed to intubate several, saving the need for operating, and with steroids and steam tent resolved the emergency later. My experience of over one thousand anaesthetics with intubations helped.

On one occasion, I was on duty at night when at 1.00 am a lady arrived with a crying baby less than a week old. She said her four hourly feeding as advised by the obstetric hospital didn't seem to be working. I asked how long it was since the last feed. It was only two or three hours. I asked her to demonstrate how she fed the baby. She did so efficiently and the baby slept soundly afterwards. I told her to continue doing the same every time the baby cried as this would solve the problem. It was, in effect, demand feeding. It also allowed me back to bed.

THE PAEDIATRIC PHYSICIANS AT P.M.H.

Perhaps the most memorable physician at Princess Margaret was Dr Ian Walman, a dynamic, hyper manic doctor and an excellent paediatrician. He would hold after-work parties in which we all learned and danced rock and roll to Bill Haley's "Rock Around the Clock", a vinyl record that we nearly wore out. Ian used to do a party trick standing on one foot on the top of a standard beer bottle. It was no mean feat of balancing.

Amongst other paediatricians of note was Dr Colin Walker, a cardiologist whom we liked so much we named our first son Colin after him. Dr Ian Lewis and another prominent fellow whose name I have forgotten were both great doctors.

I diagnosed a trachea-oesophageal fistula (T.O.F.). The child had a rare type with a single hole in the gullet communicating with the trachea, which was not diagnosed on earlier investigation. Dr Lewis asked me how I had managed to diagnose this where other doctors had failed. I said simply, "The nurse accompanying the child told me that every time the child was fed, it coughed and became respiratorily distressed, which is a classic sign of T.O.F." The history tells nine tenths of the story.

THE SURGEONS AT P.M.H.

The most impressive surgeon at PMH was Harold McComb, a paediatric plastic surgeon. He did such wonderful cleft lip and palate surgery, which so impressed and influenced me that I later became a plastic surgeon with my main sub-specialty, Cleft Lip and Palate Surgery. He operated with the child's head on his lap for best vision of the palate.

Dr Daley Smith was another excellent all round surgeon from whom I learned a lot.

Les Le Souef was a wartime surgeon who won a Croix De Guerre medal for his surgery performed on French soldiers and others in a World War II concentration camp. Les considered himself a plastic surgeon without ever having had any formal training and like a number of other post-war untrained doctors did the surgery badly. I asked Les for a reference. The one he gave me was so flowery with false claims of my skill that I never used it.

THE JUNIOR STAFF

We were all learning.

I remember a Dr. Alan Walker who was an alcoholic and never started the day without downing a bottle of beer. Another resident had a wife named Deidre, who was a former model and I think a Miss South Australia recipient. She was lovely to talk to and had an excellent technique for putting off men who were making advances towards her.

Another resident from New Zealand was a terrible diagnostician but had the good sense to refer everything on that she couldn't easily treat.

Hospital consultants told me I would make an excellent paediatrician due to my diagnostic skills but I chose a different path.

STAFF SPORTING ACTIVITIES

Superintendent Godfrey was a very good freestyle swimmer and would organise an inter-hospitals swimming carnival each year. P.M.H. usually won the 4X50 relay with Godfrey as our number one swimmer. I swam in the relay having represented medicine at Sydney University.

We also held an annual cricket match with the "consultants" versus the junior staff. The consultants usually won. I played in this match and, coming off the winter season playing hockey, had an eye for the ball, especially using the much larger cricket bat. You were allowed out twice. I partnered with our A Grade fast bowler and batsman. I couldn't decide when to run or not to run so he called from both ends. I scored 27 runs and he scored 50 or 60 runs, which was the top scoring partnership. With his first grade bowling we beat the consultants for the first time in years, after which the yearly matches were called off.

The year 1957 that I spent at Princess Margaret Hospital was my most memorable and enjoyable of all and I always treasure it in my memories.

In 1958 I managed to get the job of Registrar, Royal Perth Hospital, probably because of a good references from Princess Margaret Children's' Hospital.

Being new at Royal Perth, I was on a two in five roster looking after consultants, with on-call duties on Friday and Monday nights. This meant I went to work on Friday morning and didn't get home until Tuesday night. It was a really tough roster. We would get about five hours sleep a night and our residents' quarters had mosquitoes which tended to interrupt my sleep. I learnt a lot of useful general surgery, with some orthopaedics thrown in.

Doris had our first child at St John of God Maternity Hospital in Perth and we named her Alison Lee Walker. I encouraged Doris to breast-feed and although it wasn't so common in those days, Alison was breast fed to the age of one.

Doris' father died in mid-1958 and, sadly for Doris, we didn't have the money or time to fly back to Newcastle for his funeral.

Alison Lee Walker aged one year

Alison developed a urinary tract infection, which responded to antibiotics. I should have referred her for a urological check-up as it turned out later that she had congenitally abnormal kidneys and renal tract, which was discovered in Glasgow in 1962 when she was five years old. She had a non-functional right kidney and a hydro nephrosis (kidney swelling due to build-up of urine) with obstruction on the left with about 25% function. All this was treated later in Australia.

Doris gave birth to two more children, Colin on 10th April 1959 and David on 24th November 1960, both born at Toowoomba Hospital under Dr. Harbison.

4 TARA

EXPERIENCES AS A SOLO GENERAL PRACTITIONER IN TARA, QUEENSLAND

I made up my mind to earn some money in general practice to allow me to pursue my surgical studies. To this end, I applied for and was granted a job in Queensland as the Medical Superintendent of Tara Hospital on the Western Darling Downs area. It was a solo practice serving a population of 900 in the town of Tara and with a surrounding population of three thousand people.

The family at Tara. Doris, Alison, Colin, David and grandmother, Lydia Hyams

It was a 24/7 job. I ran a public clinic service of two hours Monday to Friday, followed by my private practice. I built a surgery building adjacent to the twelve-bed hospital serviced by a matron, a senior sister and nurses. I did all the obstetrics, sixty-five per year and sent off problem cases to Dr. Harbison at Toowoomba, two hours' drive away.

In the country, people would sometimes travel for two hours just to see you and they were not in a hurry to leave the consultation. They did not often present with trivial complaints or illnesses and were always keen to work, often running a property with no replacement during illness.

I remember one man who dropped a ton of metal bar on his great toe smashing it to bits. He asked if he could work on with a steel-capped boot, never mind the pain!

I took X-Rays and mended fractures (thanks to my Parramatta Hospital experience), repaired wounds and cleared out miscarriages. I did emergency abdominal surgery including appendectomy, ruptured ulcers, repairs and ectopic pregnancies. I had a very good obstetric trained Scottish Matron whose judgement in labour was excellent. I did forceps deliveries, manipulations and breach deliveries. My caesarean rate was extremely low as a birth was a big event for Matron who discouraged caesareans. Sixty-five births a year for three and a half years, a total over 200. I treated snakebites and veterinary injuries such as dogs cut by wild boars. Snakebites on dogs were usually fatal.

We would go kangaroo shooting at night as the roo population outnumbered the sheep in places and competed for grass.

I took up competitive rifle shooting and became quite skilful with averages that put me in the sniper category according to the A.I.F. I represented the Darling Downs District Rifle Association and each year we had a shoot-out against the other fifteen districts in Queensland, shooting for the Murray Shield, with fifteen shots for each of ten shooters. I came third in our team of ten and we won the Murray Shield that year. I was asked to join Rotary, but chose the younger Apex Club organisation. It was very helpful to me for learning public speaking.

Feral pigs were a menace in Western Queensland, destroying crops and killing lambs. One farmer used to challenge a large boar on foot using a wheat bag as a matador would. When he had the boar confused, he would jump on its back and garrotte it cutting its throat. I often received young pig meat as a present.

In Tara, it was my practice to ask for the consultation fee at the time of the visit. I allowed well-known patients like farmers and shopkeepers to run up an account and pay on a monthly basis.

A number of patients, usually farm labourers or itinerant workers would arrive telling this story: "I haven't got any money as I have just arrived in town." They often gave their address as Murphy's boarding house, and asked, "Can I pay later?" They never did. I used to see them and ask them to pay now or forget it and to not come back unless they could pay for their visit in advance. They never returned.

One clever patient working with a farmer whom I knew well, used to ring up and make an appointment, always on a Sunday morning. I charged a double fee for Sundays visits but this did not dissuade him. Sundays were usually only for urgent visits so I asked him why he always came on that day.

"I don't like taking time off work to come to the doctor." His visits were often for trivial complaints like a rash. He ran up a bill of five Sunday consultations, and when I phoned his employer, he told the farm worker had left town with no forwarding address (and probably changed his name as well). It was no wonder he came on Sundays with no waiting and free consultations!

I had a few Aboriginal patients who visited me. They often asked for money for food and unwisely I gave them about five pounds (fifty dollars or more in today's money).

"What! You didn't give Aboriginals money?" my friends said. "It will only be spent on grog."

It was a lesson learned. I should have offered them a credit for food only on my grocer's account in town, as then they could only spend the money in the correct way.

In the world today, many underdeveloped countries get large donations of millions of dollars from the West. They often buy military equipment or it lines the pockets of corrupt heads of state. If only they could have learned from my Tara experiences!

The Tara Hospital was administered by a group of five businessmen in the area. The board chairman was an ex-R.A.A.F person who thought he could rule over the doctor. He also took up rifle shooting but was never up to my standard. On Sunday mornings, I used to drive away leaving the matron in charge with instructions to send the police out to the rifle range if anything needed my advice or attention. I'd be away from the hospital for some four to six hours.

The board chairman decided I should be stopped and so visited the Director of Health in Brisbane, telling a woeful story of neglect and disaster in Tara during my absences. All lies. The Director issued me with a directive that I had to apply for leave of absence to the hospital board if I wanted to go further than fifty miles outside of town. Some of my home visits were further than this anyway. I told the board I was not complying with their directive and they could sack me. Of course, you could never sack a popular solo G.P. The board chairman had run foul of two other organisations, the municipal council and the "Gums" School having been sacked from both.

This altercation convinced me to move on and do my surgical studies in the UK. I had saved about two thousand pounds which was enough to do the courses. I put my practice up for sale and had a buyer who opted out when he heard the board was unfavourable. Tara had no doctors for two years after I left and conscripts from Brisbane serviced the town. After this, the Director of Health dissolved the Tara Board.

5 UNITED KINGDOM

TRAVEL TO THE U.K.

I worked at locums in Sydney whilst waiting for transport to the U.K., which was to be by boat on the *Castle Felice*, an Italian liner.

I had booked a primary training course in Glasgow, of twelve weeks duration with a practical section as opposed to the London FRACS course without the practical. There were no training courses available in Australia and so going overseas was the only option for me as well as for many of my colleagues.

Doris was pregnant and reluctant to come with three children but finally decided it was better than staying home.

The *Castle Felice* took five weeks voyaging Sydney to Portsmouth via Singapore and Colombo, Ceylon (now Sri Lanka). The trip was eventful in that David, aged two, fell out of the top bunk onto his head on two occasions giving himself a large lump which he still has. He also developed gastro-enteritis, which went through the whole ship. There was little in the way of infection control and virtually everyone got it. David was quite ill and a trip to the medical centre was of little help. He was given an opium draught and enteroviaform tablets, both of which were useless and contra-indicated as per my Princess

Margaret Hospital training. He recovered with careful fluid management by ourselves.

We arrived in Southampton and travelled to London where I arranged courses in Glasgow for the primary F.R.A.C. The degree in Glasgow was the F.F.P.S., Fellow of the Faculty of Physicians and Surgeons, and as such, it was not recognised as a surgical degree except by the Scots. They later changed the name to F.R.C.S. Glasgow to attract more students, which it did. I sat Part II in Edinburgh because of the F.F.P.S. name being unrecognised.

We rented a flat in Baileston on the Edinburgh side of Glasgow. The winter came with record snow in December, two feet deep outside on Christmas Day. Coming from hot sunny Queensland, we felt the cold and spent much money on coal to warm our unheated flat. It was the coldest winter in 40 years.

HEALTH PROBLEMS IN THE U.K.

After our five week sea voyage via Singapore and Colombo, Ceylon (Sri Lanka), we arrived at Southampton and moved to a hotel in London before transit to Glasgow.

I met the Dean of Glasgow University who organised my F.R.C.S. Part 1 course. As Doris was pregnant, I asked him to recommend a good obstetrician and he directed us to Professor Duck,

Head of the Obstetric Department at Stobhill Hospital.

At her first meeting with Professor Duck, Doris asked if he had private patients.

"No way" said he. "My services are free to all and cannot be bought."

He was an out and out socialist, a real academic - a term I changed to *a comedian* after ensuing events.

At her first obstetrical clinical visit, Doris lined up with fifteen other mothers and was seen by a junior doctor. So it went on each visit until about thirty-six weeks when a Registrar examined her, then another, then Professor Duck. She was told nothing and sent home. It had been noted that she had a high level of sugar in her urine at each visit.

I received a call from Professor D, who was slow to come to the point in telling me that Doris had an intrauterine death. I examined her and found no heartbeat, no movements for two days.

"Didn't they tell you?" I said.

"I don't think we could have done anything," said the Prof.

"Well, you certainly can't now." I replied.

He didn't realise I had obstetric training in Australia including sixty-five births per year in Tara. Doris should have had glucose tolerance tests and investigations for what was pre-diabetes and perhaps some closer sugar management.

Doris had an uncomplicated still-birth attended to by the junior staff, with no Prof. D. His services were unavailable to the world. So much for his free services! British socialist medicine did not impressed us.

After we moved from Glasgow to Manchester, Doris was pregnant with twins. The chief obstetrician, a Dr. Walker, had her now diabetes managed by the medical staff. This amounted to frequent urine sugar tests and attempts to control her sugar levels. She was hospitalised for five weeks before term in an attempt to control the diabetes.

At full term delivery the babies died during birth, a boy and a girl. Unfortunately, the type of blood sugar testing which gives a very accurate control of diabetes had not yet been introduced, being some five to ten years in the future. Doris was pregnant when we arrived back in Australia in 1968 and the baby girl died of respiratory failure at 22 hours post-delivery. This condition, in which the lungs fill with fluid, was successfully treated by intensive care about six months later. We were just too early.

ALISON LEE WALKER

Alison had an asthma attack, which took her to hospital where they found she had an obstructive renal disease with no function on one side and about one quarter in the other kidney. She had an operation to relieve a hydronephrosis, which did little, as it was too late.

On return to Australia, she subsequently went into renal failure at age twelve and after one and a half years on dialysis and two transplants, she died of a complication about five weeks after her second transplant. We missed our beautiful little daughter terribly but were comforted knowing she awaits the resurrection.

MY ASTHMA

in Scotland, at age thirty-three, I developed asthma. This was partly due to the air pollution in Glasgow, and partly due to an inherent tendency from my mother, an asthmatic. My sister Joyce had it quite severely. I was treated with *Ventolin* for attacks and a *spinhaler* for prevention but my asthma has continued to the present day. I did exercise in the form of long distance running, hockey and in Australia, swimming. All of that tended to keep me fit.

In 2003, I developed a severe chest infection which was treated by the G.P. with antibiotics. When I wasn't getting any better after six weeks, I consulted my physician, Dr Jack Fowler. He found I had obstructive airways and pneumonia. He put me on steroids and a high-powered antibiotic. The condition settled but with a residual bronchial tube dilation in the form of mild bronchiectasis. This produces an accumulation of bronchial secretions, which cause me to cough frequently.

STUDY FOR THE F.F.P.S

The primary F.F.P.S. course was twelve weeks long with study in the basic sciences - anatomy, physiology and biochemistry. The exam was held just a week after completion of the course. I had done insufficient study in the lead up to the exam and was hopelessly, inadequately prepared. I sat mainly for experience and failed all three subjects as expected.

I decided I needed tuition in anatomy and asked the Anatomy Department of Glasgow University for a tutor, which they supplied. I took two hours tutoring in one session per week. I asked the tutor to give me a viva voce test on anatomy specimens covering one twelfth of the anatomy course as selected by me, this being the exam format. I met the Professor, Head of Department almost every session for twelve weeks.

In the exam, there was the professor examining me! He had the leg of a cadaver exposed and after I had correctly and promptly identified about eight to ten parts, he turned to the clinical co-examiner and said, "Do you want to bother asking him any questions?" It was the best exam I had ever passed.

After gaining the F.R.C.S. Part 1, I looked for a job in surgery. I applied for fifteen jobs at registrar level only to receive one interview. At this, I was told I was far and above the most experienced candidate but the job had already been given to a local in-house doctor.

I applied for a lower level Senior House Officer post at Hairmyers Hospital on the outskirts of Glasgow at East Kilbride.

The Chief, sitting at his desk, said, "You've got the job but you are far too experienced for it, but we can guarantee a registrar post in six months, if you will take it."

I was given a choice of two out of six specialties to work at, one in each of the two three month periods before taking the registrar job. I chose chest surgery and urology, which gave me some useful training in these areas.

My registrar post was a one in two roster with a South African surgeon, "Mr." Samuels who was quite experienced. We did four to five emergency surgeries per day and I became quite a well-trained general surgeon. In my first week on call, I asked my Chief, "What I should do with a case I can't diagnose?"

"Phone the consultant for advice." I did this and the advice was usually to take the patient to theatre and do an exploratory laparotomy.

"What if I can't handle it?" I asked.

"Then ring the consultant again."

I was getting what was known as the "yo yo" treatment. *You are on your own!* After a time one soon learned to be self-reliant, and no longer called the consultant.

The consultants were all very experienced and skilful surgeons except for one, a Mr. Clark, who although a good operator, lacked in diagnostic skills such that I caught him out on several occasions. A sixty-year-old patient was admitted to the medical ward with a diagnosis of gastroenteritis and severe dehydration, which is rare in sixty-year-olds. The Resident asked me to see him and put up an IV to correct his dehydration. An abdominal X-Ray showed classical of obstruction and he had an untreated inguinal hernia. Mr. Clark decided he might have had an obstructed hernia now corrected. The patient deteriorated over the next day or so and the resident (our Chief's son) asked me what to do next. I suggested, "Get your father to see the patient."

The chief examined the patient and said, "Silly bugger!" He phoned Mr. Clark and ordered, "Get the patient to surgery a.s.a.p. and fix his obstruction."

Mr. Clark called me an "impudent puppy" for having caught him out on several occasions. Mr. Douglas, however, was an excellent surgeon from whom I learnt a lot.

Burns patients were referred to Royal Glasgow Infirmary's Burns Unit for treatment. In the course of such management, a registrar, Ian Jackson, came to our hospital to graft a burn.

"Want a job in plastic surgery?" he asked.

I told him I was near the end of my contract and after thinking for three seconds, replied, "Yes."

STUDY FOR PART II F.R.C.S.

I took a correspondence course for Part II of the F.R.C.S. It consisted of weekly exam papers edited by a tutor. I booked an exam test for F.R.C.S. Edinburgh before I had finished my correspondence course and still had one third or more to finish. Needless to say, I failed largely because of the written papers, rather than clinical exam but I considered the exam a good trial run.

I booked the next exam to follow and the chief thoracic surgeon at our hospital contacted me to pass on some tips for the exam. He had been an examiner for the F.R.C.S. Edinburgh for fifteen years. At the meeting, he spoke for half an hour telling me all the trick questions asked by all the examiners. This proved extremely useful because one of the trickiest questions on the management of a cut ureter following a hysterectomy was presented to me. There was no section on this management in our textbooks. You had to search for the answer, which I had done. My answers surprised the examiners. The rest of the exam went smoothly and I received the award of Fellow of the Royal College of Surgeons, Edinburgh in May 1965. I continued my general surgery job at Hairmyres until I started my first year as a plastics registrar at Glasgow Royal Infirmary.

I asked my boss, Mr. Macrossan, for a reference for the plastics job and he asked, "Do you want the job?"

I replied, "Yes,"

He said. "I'll see that you get it.

Mr. Tough (the head of the plastics unit) and I worked together for five years during the war." He made an appointment for me with Mr. Tough next day and I was shown over the unit and told I had the job. This time I was the local boy and the other applicants missed out.

The job at Glasgow Royal involved a lot of head and neck cancer plus facial injuries (shared with the oral surgery department), as well as burns and hand injuries. Unfortunately no cleft lips and palates. I learned a lot of basic plastic surgery techniques and was pleased with the experiences.

Unfortunately, there was no ongoing job for me in plastics. To do so they sought a job for me to work in Newcastle-on-Tyne. An advertisement appeared in the journal rather earlier than expected and I put in an application. At the interview I was asked many devious and tricky questions about why I wanted to be a plastic surgeon. After a long delay, it was announced that I came second and a Cardiff S.H.O. got the job. He was obviously the best candidate. We found out later that the job had been rigged and promised by the plastics chief via a Cardiff contact to be given to the other candidate. It is likely he had trouble convincing the board.

A job came up a week or so later in Manchester, for which I applied, not knowing there was still a job offering in Newcastle. I presented to Manchester. The chief, a Mr. Champion, was an Australian. As I approached the desk, he said, "You're the best candidate and the other three are all black, so do you want the job?" I took it. The Newcastle job offer came some three weeks later but I was no longer interested.

Manchester turned out to be a good position and we did all the cleft surgery for the five million people in our area. This was very useful for my subsequent career in Newcastle, N.S.W. We did burns, hand injuries, facial injuries and some cosmetic surgery, which included breast reductions and rhinoplasty, as our chief Mr. Randall Champion was E.N.T. trained and he taught me to do a sub mucous resection of the nasal septum. He also taught us how to do cosmetic rhinoplasty operations, all of which was very useful in my subsequent private practice in New South Wales.

At a hand-surgery meeting in London, I met a Sydney plastic surgeon, Dr. Sweeney. There had been an advertisement for a plastic surgeon for Newcastle N.S.W. some months before and I asked him who got the job. He told me it was a Dr. Emmett but he was offered a further year's training in Auckland, New Zealand. He relinquished his Newcastle appointment. I wrote to Newcastle asking for a job in plastic surgery and was told I could be appointed but only if I was resident in Newcastle. They clearly didn't want another disappointment. I replied that I would be returning to live in Newcastle in May 1968. I received the appointment on 14th May 1968, my birthday.

At the board interview, they asked if I could do cleft lip and palate surgery. I replied in the affirmative but was asked how well I can do them. "Who am I to judge my results?" I asked. "I was in Manchester for two years and we did one hundred and twenty operations per year. I must have learned something." The interviewers asked no further questions.

The reason behind these questions was that in the early days, cleft surgery was done somewhat badly by general practitioners and an E.N.T surgeon, Dr. Watson, took over. He went to London to study under Dr. Dennis Browne at Great Ormond Street Hospital for six weeks. A patient who had her lip repaired told me he re-did her operation after his trip to the U.K. now having learnt how to do it properly. He moved to Sydney for his children's education some three years before I came and before moving, showed his partner Dr. E. Egan how to do the operation on one lip and one palate.

Dr. E. Egan was a somewhat ham-fisted surgeon and did badly, so much so that others took up the challenge. I saw one lip-patient operated on by the head orthopaedic surgeon. A number of cleft palate patients arrived at age twelve for palate repair. "You could have come at age two years!" I said. But the E.N.T. surgeon was making such a mess of palate repair that they were advised to present for surgery at age twelve when they were older and hopefully she would have moved on by then. I operated on them all, doing lip surgery at three months and palates at one year, which I shortened to nine months in later years as the earlier operation gave better speech results.

Dr. John Newton started practice in Newcastle in the early 1980s and was keen to do cleft surgery so we shared operations plus our third world surgery. I attended all cleft surgery meetings and read up all journals becoming quite knowledgeable on the subject and my surgical results improved over the years.

I was also interested in speech problems following cleft palate repair and investigated Velato Palatal Insufficiency (V.P.I.) in which the patient had a cleft speech due to nasal air escape. My son, Colin, did the radiology (palate fluoroscopy) and I learnt and did palate nasal endoscopy. Together with speech therapist assessment, we had a pretty good analysis of the speech problems and could do "pharyngo-plasties", i.e. surgical correction of the palate defect.

On my first visit to Peru in 2004, I was the only surgeon of the three of us who could do the secondary speech corrections with pharyngo-plasty. On retirement I considered myself as a cleft surgeon, this being my sub-speciality and area of main interest.

6 NEWCASTLE, AUSTRALIA

PLASTIC SURGERY

In June 1968, having been appointed to all the hospitals in the Newcastle area, I set up private practice in Hunter Street, Newcastle. I saw one patient in the first week and business was so slow I decided to do locum G.P. work to earn some money. I had six weeks with the Smith Street, Charlestown practice with Bill Charleton and Paddy Lightfoot. It proved to be an interesting six weeks.

My outpatient sessions at Royal Newcastle Hospital were twice a week and within a few months I was seeing forty patients, together with one operating session at Royal Newcastle and one a week at the Mater where I did my cleft surgery on children. I also did operation sessions at Belmont and Wallsend Hospitals.

The patients seen were any with skin loss, burns, traumatic injuries, congenital abnormalities of the urethra (hypospadias), syndactylys of the hands (webbed fingers), head and neck cancers. I treated patients that had failed surgery and we did scar contractures. We re-did hypospadias and some revision of previous cleft lip and palate surgery. Surprisingly enough, older palate patients with an anterior fistula, were more concerned with leakage through the nose than with any speech defects which they said were understood by friends and relatives and so presented no problems. I was able to fix them all.

I treated all burns at Royal Newcastle for fifteen years until the State Government decided to centralise burn management at the Royal North Shore and Concord hospitals in Sydney. I had one 80% body burn survivor and used cadaver skin as a temporary dressing in large burns to good effect.

I was also asked to treat open compound fractures of legs and hands, which was done with flap repairs. Some long-standing ulcerations from trauma were also effectively treated, with compliments from the local surgical staff. I also treated head and neck cancer and became a foundation member of the Mater Hospital Head and Neck Cancer Group.

John Newton came to practise in Newcastle as a plastic surgeon and I learnt microsurgery from him as well as doing a couple of courses in Sydney. I practised on chickens from Steggles, operating at the Mater Hospital using their microscope.

In the early 1970s, Doris and I flew to Madrid to attend a meeting of the European section of the International Society of Plastic Surgeons. While we were there, we immersed ourselves in Spanish culture, especially music and dancing.

Doris and Bill in Madrid

THE MARGARET ILUKOL STORY

Margaret Ilukol was a nomadic native of the KARIMOJONG tribe of Northern Uganda. Her tribe moved from one food source to another sleeping in makeshift huts, tents or out in the open.

In March 1963 at aged eight or nine years (birth dates are not recorded in tribal Africa) she was attacked one night by a hyena, a large dog-like creature which bites the face off victims. Margaret was dragged away from the camp about a mile distant and found next day by her relatives. She had a shocking injury with most of her central face bitten off; the nose, both lips and adjacent cheeks, mainly the right side, the anterior parts of

77

both upper and lower jaws and part of her scalp. She had almost died from blood loss.

She was taken to a nearby village at Loroyo awaiting further transport to Moroto town. A passing road repair truck was able to transport her to the nearest hospital at Moroto, together with her father and mother. There she received some medical treatment now five days after the injury.

She recalls being shunned by everyone because of the smell of dead flesh and having green flies feasting on her face with the inevitable maggots crawling all over her. As well, some people were horrified after looking at her facial wound and would look away, some throwing up.

Moroto Hospital had two beds and two doctors and was basically a first aid station doing basic care. She was told she would have to be sent to Mulago Hospital in Kampala, the main hospital in Uganda with 2000 beds.

Margaret was admitted to a ward for the most serious cases of trauma, cancer and advanced disease. It had a high death rate. The first treatment was cleaning the wound and feeding her to build up strength to withstand an anaesthetic and operations. Initially she had multiple debridement operations removing dead flesh and bone with removal of teeth. She was also given a long course of antibiotics. The wound was closed with skin grafts before any reconstructive operations were undertaken.

She received treatment from Dr. P. Shepherd, a visiting general surgeon from Australia, who although not a trained plastic surgeon, did his best using plastic surgery techniques. Dr. Knight and Dr. Arnold Bisase treated her facio-maxillary injury in the facio-maxillary unit. After the wound was healed they had a prosthetic facial mask with false teeth made for her to wear and she was able to move around the hospital. She had to learn the local languages and English.

Artist's impression of Margaret's injuries

She learned dressing techniques from the nursing staff and in particular, how to suck out a tracheostomy to clear an airway. On one occasion, a small child gasping for breath with an obstruction presented to the hospital. The nursing staff was temporarily absent. Margaret successfully sucked out the tracheostomy, clearing the airway, much to the commendation of the staff. She said she realised at that point in time that she would like to be a nurse to help people as her life's ambition.

At Kampala, she had pedicle procedures to reconstruct the large hole in her central face, one from the shoulder via an arm attachment, and later a bulkier abdominal tube pedicle moved in stages to the face. There were many adjustment operations. There was also treatment for an exposed right eye due to skin and lower eyelid loss, which had resulted in a large degree of partial blindness of her right eye.

Margaret received basic education in two schools by local teachers and learned to read and write. She was educated to about an Australian ten-year-old level. She received instruction in the Christian religion and was baptised by an Anglican minister and given the names of her tutor, Margaret Rosalind (Ilukol) as she had no tribal names.

She remained in Kampala Mulago Hospital and boarding schools for the next four years and plans to send her overseas for further surgery were put on hold due to the country's political instability caused by President Idi Amin.

An occupational therapist, Nightingale Kalinda, wrote an article about Margaret's plight that

Rotary International magazine published. She titled it, *A New Face for Margaret*. This resulted in twelve international Rotary applications offering help.

The application by Kevin Leary of Toronto NSW Rotary Club was successful on the basis that all treatment by hospitals, doctors (me) and billeting with Rotarians would be free with no need to raise large funds, which was the requirement of all the other applications.

Kevin and Val Leary and daughter went out to Kampala in December 1974 and escorted Margaret back to Australia somewhat without her full consent or detailed consultation.

I first met Margaret on 17th December 1974. She was a shy, timid girl by then of about eighteen years. She said nothing. She wore a mask to cover her face. She had what amounted to two large fatty tube pedicles covering a large defect and placed horizontally, the gap between them representing her mouth. There had been no attempt at nasal construction and the front half of her whole nasal cavity was missing. I could see that her reconstruction represented an enormous challenge as few surgeons ever get to treat an injury like this because mostly the victims die of blood loss. We were in uncharted territory navigating our way.

I firstly did operations taking fat out of the lips making them a more normal size. A lower jaw shortening and realignment operation followed this, which greatly improved her facial balance. I then did several nasal reconstruction operations with staged tube pedicles, cartilage framework and adjustments.

Sadly, even though one could get a reasonably natural looking nose, with the passage of time it would atrophy (shrink) due to poor blood and nerve supply. This would also block the nasal airway. Margaret said all she wanted was the ability to breathe through her nose. I removed the nasal construction.

Lyn Thorpe with Margaret Ilukol

I sent her to the oro-facio maxillary unit in Melbourne for manufacture of a nasal prosthesis as they made the best in Australia. I was amazed how good it looked mounted on her glasses. You would hardly know it was false. She came back to Newcastle and had two copies made by our local dental department at Newcastle Hospital.

In 1976, Lochinvar Catholic College accepted her as a student and despite numerous interruptions for surgery, Margaret completed her HSC although her marks were low due to all the surgery interfering with her studies. She enjoyed her stay there and joined in all activities including playing hockey. Because she had no active muscles in her lips, she could not use them to speak. By using her tongue to phonate, however, her ability to communicate without using her lips worked surprisingly well.

Because of her poor speech and facial defect, she had trouble finding a hospital that would take her on as a nursing trainee but with help from higher nursing staff and some newspaper advertisements, Gosford Hospital accepted her as a trainee nurse starting on 26th May 1980. She completed her training and passed her final examination on 25th February 1984. She obtained a position as a full time nurse night sister at Royal Newcastle Hospital.

On 20th April 1985, the Rotary Club of Toronto held a Rotary District dinner, at which they awarded me a Paul Harris Fellowship, which is quite a high Rotary honour. All the Rotary dignitaries were there and they screened a television-taped message of congratulations by the Rotary International President. I hadn't realised how important my contribution to "A New Face for Margaret" had been. I became a Rotarian six years later.

Margaret made three trips back to Uganda to visit her family and the Karimojong tribe but found she was now too westernised to return to the nomadic tribal life. Her parents died of cholera some years later.

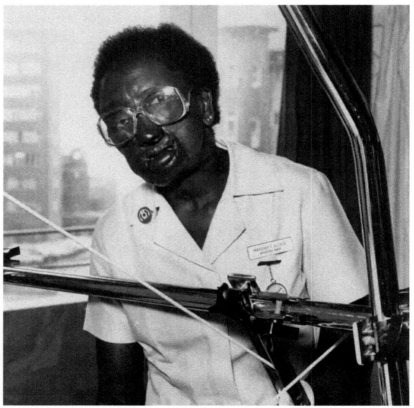
Nurse Margaret Ilukol

Margaret continued as a night superintendent at Royal Newcastle and John Hunter Hospitals until, in March 2015, she had an unfortunate accident at home. Under the influence of alcohol, she fell down a full flight of stairs and asphyxiated at the bottom being found dead a few days later. In her will she left her estate of approximately a million dollars to Rotary District 9670 (spanning the Rotary Clubs of Newcastle and to the west), the Rotarians of which, myself included, had given her a new face with which she was able to face the world. She recorded her life story in a 1990 book titled *Child of the Karimojong*.

Margaret was the most interesting patient of my entire surgical career.

THE HISTORY OF CLEFT SURGERY IN NEWCASTLE

When I arrived in Newcastle in 1968, most of the cleft palate patients were referred to Sydney for management under Dr. Day at the Children's' Hospital, Camperdown. General practitioners performed the Surgery early on with poor results until Ear Nose and Throat surgeon, Dr. Watson, decided to take them on. I arranged a visit to Dr. D. Day, paediatric cleft surgeon, to see his surgical technique on clefts. He was doing good work. I asked him how he repaired palate fistulae and he replied, "I never get any!" Well, the nurse or mother obviously must have caused the fistulae I saw after his surgery. My opinion of Dr. Day went down after that.

One of my patients came from the Philippines for cleft repair on the recommendation of a fellow

Philippino working as a lecturer at Newcastle University.

My own cleft surgery improved with time and with the experience of extra cases done overseas through the Australian Interplast Charity and others.

I performed operating sessions at West Wallsend and Belmont Hospitals. West Wallsend, a smaller hospital, was the most efficient and economical hospital in the Hunter Region, as a result of which it was closed down and used as a rehab unit in the rationalisation of Hunter Area Health Board!

My operating sessions at Belmont were on a Thursday from 1:00pm to 5:00pm. The staff anaesthetist would not let you start a long case after 4pm and the anaesthetist would literally stop at 5pm. One had to adjust the list to fit in with this arrangement. I used to go to Belmont Golf Club once a fortnight for a golf lesson with Paul Robinson after my hospital operating session.

It took at least six months for the general medical profession to realise what a plastic surgeon could do and referrals came slowly. I did the full range of plastic surgery: congenital deformities, cleft lips and palates, hypospadias (where the urethra is relocated in a male baby's penis) - including revision of failed hypospadias, syndactyls (webbed fingers) of the hands, head and neck cancer and all forms of trauma including facial injuries. The Oromaxilliary Department managed facial fractures.

One of my first patients was a pensioner requesting a face lift. I enquired as to how she was going to pay for this. She told me she was selling a block of land to cover costs. She failed to pay up and finished up in the magistrate's court. He allotted $50 per week to be paid to me until the debt was covered. I received two payments only and couldn't be bothered chasing the rest. I learnt an important lesson: asking for payment before cosmetic surgery operations.

7 BREAST SURGERY

BREAST AUGMENTATION

I had seen only one breast augmentation operation done in Manchester before returning home to Newcastle. My first such patient in Newcastle was a small flat chested woman. I implanted the smallest Dow Corning prostheses made at the time. They were really too big for her and only later Dow Corning made a wider range of prostheses including smaller ones.

The silicon gel in the prostheses had an adverse reaction causing scar tissue to form around the prosthesis resulting in it becoming hard (sometimes rock hard) giving the prosthesis a sharp rim-like appearance that was obviously an implant. At least thirty percent of patients had this problem with their prosthetics.

An American surgeon noted that a patient's partner could break the contracted capsule by forcibly squeezing the breast between the two palms of the hands. This "crunch" ruptured the capsular contraction and softened the breast. It was an alternative to an open operation incising the capsule. I performed an experiment, crunching the prostheses and then operating to see what happened inside. Not surprisingly, many prostheses ruptured, with silicon gel extruding widely even into the axilla (armpit). I published the results of ten cases and recommended that the "crunch" technique be abandoned.

I operated on a number of transsexual men doing a bilateral augmentation. This posed a problem for the private hospital staff as to which ward they should be housed: male or female, and which toilet should they use? They usually finished up solo in a private room.

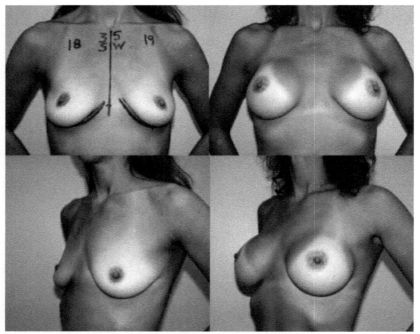

Breast Augmentation (By Courtesy of Dr.Ron Gemberling)

One transsexual lady from Singleton was running a hair dressing salon and told me money was no problem for paying the costs. She failed to pay up.

I made a telephone call to the post office and the Post Master said, "You and fourteen other businesses would like to know where 'she' has gone."

A Go-Go dancer from Kings Cross, the notorious sex centre of Sydney, came for an operation. She requested minimal scarring as she danced topless for the public. I did a trans-nipple approach as she had big areolas and I achieved a virtually scar-free result. At operation, I found she hadn't paid for the surgery, claiming her mother had failed to front up with my fee.

The dancer never paid me and I considered going down to her go-go dancing show in Kings Cross and calling out, "Those boobs are not hers. They are mine and she didn't pay for them!"

I have since insisted on payment of surgeon's fees before giving a booking date as the only sure way of collecting.

Augmentation mammoplasty operations proved to be the most satisfying in the whole range of cosmetic procedures. I had more kisses from patients than any other cosmetic procedure.

One patient stopped me in the hospital corridor with the statement, "Me and the other two girls you did breast operations on would like to *race you off.*"

I laughed. She was a 'swinger' involved in partner swopping.

The modern breast prostheses have a new gel, which is less reactive and has a very low contractive rate with much better results.

A patient in her late forties, older than usual, came and asked to have a breast augmentation. "You see, it's on account of my son's mice."

I failed to see a connection between the two until she explained.

"I have been filling my bras with cotton wool for years. My son pinches my cotton wool for his mice leaving me in trouble. So I have decided to have a breast augmentation."

She certainly needed that, so I did it.

BREAST REDUCTION SURGERY

Patients with over-large breasts have several complaints. They get undue, unwanted attention from the male sex, sometimes with derogatory comments; they have difficulty engaging in active sports and their breasts flop about; their breasts also droop excessively sometimes as far as the navel; they often have a dorsal backache due to the stooping posture and sometimes a rash in the sub-mammary fold underneath the breasts.

In Manchester, we were doing a Swedish breast reduction operation devised by Stromberg. The operation tended to have problems with necrosis (death of a piece of tissue) of the nipple and soon we replaced it with operations that created fewer nipple problems.

I did an operation devised by Robbins with good results. It was necessary to warn patients about the possible degree of scarring as some patients formed thick scars and could sue you if not pre-warned. I would illustrate the scarring and possible thickness for the patient and consequently, no one ever sued me.

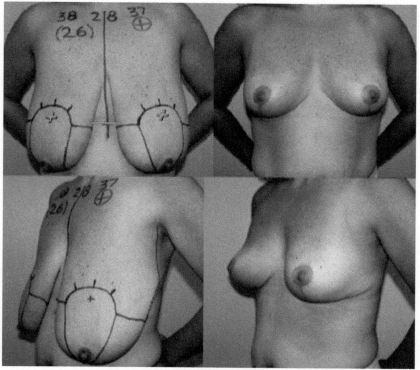

Breast Reduction (By Courtesy of Dr. Ron Gemberling)

There were a number of variations of operations mainly aimed at minimising the extent of scarring. Mostly patients were very satisfied with their results with a better appearance, uplift and a relief of symptoms.

One surgeon, Dr Terry Gallagher, gave a talk on the variation in appearance of breasts with names such as *microboobia* (small breasts), *macroboobia* (very large breasts), *droopiboobia* (droopy breasts), *razorstrapboobia* (long thin droopy breasts) and others accompanied by slides. It was always a winner as a talk.

BREAST RECONSTRUCTION AFTER MASTECTOMY

In more recent times, patients who have had a total mastectomy (breast removal) for cancer have been offered a reconstruction operation as opposed to wearing a prosthesis in the bra.

The simplest operation was to implant a silicon prosthesis replacing the removed breast together with a reduction/uplift of the adjacent breast to achieve symmetry.

Occasionally, we needed an inflatable tissue expander to stretch the skin and enable a sizeable prosthesis to be implanted (usually after several months of gradual expansion of the cavity) This worked very well and I did lots of them.

With the advent of microsurgery, a number of local flaps can be used to replace the removed breast(s). The commonest was a so-called "tram" flap (trans-abdomino-muscular skin flap) which involved the removal of a lower abdominal flap of skin and fat on a muscle pedicle swung up to fill the breast cavity. It was an effective flap but left a scarred abdomen.

Another flap was the latissimus dorsi flap in which a large area of skin and fat was pedicalised and brought forward from the back to the breast cavity. This gave an effective breast replacement but left a large scapula scar, which was not very cosmetic either, and virtually all of my patients when shown photographs of the scar, elected not to have this operation.

All breast implant operations ran the risk of haematoma (blood collection) and extrusion with wound breakdown. As well, you could not always get complete breast symmetry so I warned patients of these complications.

Recently a number of surgeons have been doing immediate breast reconstruction at the time of mastectomy with good results. This early operation has a higher complication rate requiring a redo, and many patients do not accept the less than normal reconstruction compared with those patients who have no breast for a time before undertaking repair.

NIPPLE RECONSTRUCTION

It is possible to use a number of local flaps of breast skin to give a projecting nipple. They have one major disadvantage in that the projecting nipple tends to atrophy and shrink with time and they become flat. I had my maxillary dental department make a silicon prosthetic stick-on nipple which was a simple and more effective replacement and worked well for many of my patients. I wrote a paper on this.

There are many variations possible with each patient and radiotherapy is often a factor in choice of treatment.

BREAST-FEEDING

My mother breast-fed all her children as her only form of contraception and she breast-fed me for nearly two years. In my medical practice, I promoted breast-feeding as the best form of nutrition for babies.

In Tara, Western Queensland, I had two mothers having their fifth child who had never breast fed before but wanted to this time. With counselling and the help of the obstetric trained hospital matron, who also knew how to teach the breast-feeding technique, we managed to get these two mothers to breast-feed their babies for six months. They were so pleased.

Whilst waiting in Sydney for my ship journey to London to study surgery, I was working as a locum for about six weeks. I had a call from a mother who had given birth about a week earlier and was having trouble establishing her breast-feeding. She said the baby was crying and wouldn't last the four hours recommended by the hospital. Her mother-in-law was pushing to have the child put on the bottle and they were in conflict.

I immediately told her to feed on demand, every hour if needed, and the milk supply would increase and the feeding times of the baby would lengthen out. She phoned me up twenty-four hours later to say I had cured the problem and she had told her mother-in-law where to go!

I was on night duty at Princess Margaret Hospital for Children in Perth, Western Australia when I was called to outpatients to see a mother who had an eight-day-old baby crying. The baby was breast-fed but the mother said she could not wait out the four-hour long interval between feeds as recommended by the hospital on discharge. I asked the mother to feed the baby for me and twenty minutes later the baby dropped off the breast sound asleep.

I told her, "You have the answer. When the baby cries, *feed it."*

This view supports the premise that feeding on demand increases milk supply and lengthens times between feeding.

My niece, Joyce Chivas, was having her third child, Anne K. and had had difficulty feeding with the first two children. I gave her a talk in hospital, pointing out how to overcome difficulties and mentioning several important facts.

1) In the animal kingdom, if babies are not breast-fed they will die but mostly don't. Are you less clever than a cow?

2) If you are a farmer and want your cow to win a prize as the best milk producer you empty their udders three times a day and not two to maximise the milk quantity.

3) Mother's breast milk is best for baby, is of the right formula and stimulates the immune system with no allergies.

4) Breast-fed babies are much less liable to get gastroenteritis and child obesity.

5) Breast-feeding is far less trouble than bottle-feeding. It does not cause drooping of the breasts although repeated pregnancies do alter the virginal breast shape.

I not only cured Joyce's difficulties but also those of the woman in the next bed!

THE NESTLÉ STORY

Nestlé, in their marketing push, offered all African women whose babies were born in hospital, free formula and bottles to get mothers to do it the "western way". The result was that after leaving hospital with baby on the bottle, the breast milk supply had dried up. These African women were too poor to buy enough formula for their baby and watered the formula down. This resulted in starvation of the child. After more than fifteen deaths Nestlé were called to account and eventually stopped the practise of free formula and bottles for post-natal mothers. Nestlé knew what they were doing but showed no morality in their business crimes.

In the western world today, many mothers choose not to breast-feed and adopt bottle-feeding early at the slightest sign of difficulty. Frequently their mothers never succeeded and passed their failure on to their daughters.

Breast-feeding requires relaxation and to just let it flow. If a mother is tense she will "hold back" and the baby will have difficulty. It requires practise in technique and relaxation. If a mother has decided to breast-feed then, with help, she will succeed. If she has decided it is too difficult, she will most probably fail sooner or later. It is all in the mind.

There are many books available on how to breast-feed and there are societies for breast-feeding mothers for those that want them. For today's working mothers, breast-feeding can be inconvenient, interfering with one's career or work so the adoption of bottle-feeding allows the mother more time.

There are so many advantages to breast-feeding, many only just being discovered by the scientific world.

SOME INTERESTING ANECDOTES

EXAMINATION OF A MOLE

It was and I guess still is a practice of teenagers to wear tight blue jeans to enhance their body shape. In the days before pre-shrunk jeans, to make them fit even tighter they would soak them in water and let them shrink on the body. One fourteen-year-old young lady arrived with her mother who asked me to examine some moles on her daughters bottom. Having completed the examination the patient couldn't pull up her shrunken jeans to get them back on. I used all my force to get them up and with a large safety pin at belt level partially saved the day with mother castigating her daughter as they left.

EXHIBITIONISM

One meets the occasional woman "flasher" who will expose more of her nude body than is asked.

A lady came in wearing a full length Kaftan robe. She wanted me to examine her moles and on request to undress pulled open the full length of her dress revealing a completely naked body underneath. I tried not to look surprised. I can only surmise she may have once been to a dermatologist who examined all of her skin.

DIFFICULT DIAGNOSTIC PROBLEMS

In medical school, the Dean of the Faculty of Medicine was Professor Charles George Lambie, a Scotsman. Together with Professor Jean Armitage, they wrote a book called "Clinical Diagnostic Method" aka 'Lambie and Armitage'. Professor Lambie lectured us for two hours each week and took six weeks to do history taking in diagnosis. He said you could diagnose ninety percent of all illnesses from the history alone and the other ten percent on examination. Clinical tests were just an addendum to confirm the diagnosis you have already made.

I am amazed these days that when a patient arrives at the E.R. (Emergency Room) almost the first thing that is done is a battery of tests and X-Rays, with what appears to be little attention to history and examination. In my early days of medicine, we did not have ultrasound, MR.Is, CT Scans, X-Rays, endoscopy and a large number of blood tests, which are now done almost as routine on patients coming to hospital. As a result, we had to rely on our clinical skills alone. I reckon I had seeing eyes on the end of my fingers.

In Third World countries, they can't afford the expensive examinations done in the west and so rely on clinical skills. In Mozambique, I was told you don't do an X-Ray unless absolutely necessary and only if it is likely to change your course of treatment. M.R.I.s and C.T.s are almost never done.

In Hairmyres Hospital near Glasgow, I told my chief about Professor Lambie and when we had a different diagnosis, he would say, "Do a Lambie on that patient and see what you can find." Success often followed.

I had one patient with shoulder pain referred by her G.P. to an orthopaedic surgeon. There was no cause for pain in the shoulder and the surgeon thought she may have gall bladder pain referred to the shoulder and so she was referred to the surgical department where I saw her. A "Lambie" type examination revealed that the pain was angina coming from the heart and referred to the shoulder. An ECG or heart beat tracing proved she had had a heart attack and was thus referred to cardiac physicians for treatment.

Another patient was admitted with "renal pain" and a front to back routine chest X-Ray was normal. On careful history taking, I found the pain was not renal but rather pleural or chest pain. She was a smoker and I had learned in the thoracic unit that you should always take a lateral (side ways) X-Ray on all chest patients. A lateral chest X-Ray revealed a carcinoma of the lung hiding behind the heart and not seen on a front only X-Ray. The chest surgeons treated the patient.

Many other cases brought my diagnostic skills to the fore, thanks to "Prof Lambie".

ACOUSTIC NEUROMA

As a GP working in Tara, Western Queensland, you saw many interesting and unusual or rare cases. I had one lady in her fifties who complained of headaches and nausea. I treated her symptomatically without effect and found she was deaf in one ear. I sent her off to the nearest ENT surgeon in Toowoomba who said she might have an acoustic neuroma - a tumour causing nerve deafness. He gave her a sedative to correct her nausea but I had already found that this didn't work, so I referred her to a neurosurgeon. She had the tumour removed but developed clotting in her major brain venous (vein) system and died of this post-operative complication.

When working as a general surgical registrar at Hairmyers Hospital, East Kilbride, I had a patient admitted with recurrent nausea and vomiting with a GP diagnosis of partial bowel obstruction. My junior Resident Medical Officer thought the patient might have liver disease and ordered blood tests, which were all negative. I had noted that she had morning vomiting, a sign of cerebral (brain) irritation.

"Let's look at the nervous system," I suggested to the junior.

Sure enough, she had deafness in one ear and her tongue poked out sideways due to pressure on the hypoglossal nerve to the tongue muscles. I made a diagnosis of a cerebello-pontine-angle tumour, the commonest one being an acoustic neuroma.

"I have never had a registrar make a diagnosis like that in my thirty-five years of surgery," said my chief, Dr Macrossan. "We had better get a physician to check it."

Privately I thought, "You can get one hundred physicians to check it but I will still be correct."

The patient was referred to a neurosurgeon who removed her acoustic neuroma but unluckily enough she also had a venous thrombosis (vein clots) in her brain and died of the complication. The neurosurgeon sent me a letter noting that it was a pity she hadn't seen me five months earlier. We might have saved her.

2. BLEEDING OESOPHAGEAL VARICES

I saw a small child aged about fifteen months with vague abdominal symptoms. On inspection, we found him to have an enlarged liver, cause unknown. I sent him to a local paediatrician in

Toowoomba, Queensland, who said the liver was not abnormally enlarged and that most probably he suffered from anaemia from mosquito bites. No specialist treatment would be required. I disagreed with the specialist's opinion about the size of the liver, having done my years of paediatric training in Perth, W.A. examining many small children's abdomens. I also saw many children with mosquito bites and a normal liver.

The child subsequently developed oesophageal varices (varicose veins of the gullet) which enlarge to accommodate blocked venous blood flow in the liver. He bled one night and I made the diagnosis, set up a drip and sent the child to Brisbane Children's Hospital. He survived the bleeding and had a surgical interruption of the gullet by means of an oesophageal gastric disconnection procedure. This amounts to cutting through the lower gullet from the stomach, tying off all the veins and re-suturing the gullet back to the stomach.

The paediatric department expressed surprise that a country GP could make such a diagnosis. I left before the child had further problems but no doubt, his liver failure would catch up with him in time. I never found out what happened to him.

3. QUINSY

Quinsy is a term for recurrent severe tonsillitis, usually in adults who have had recurrent bouts of tonsillitis, never having had their tonsils removed.

It was a common practise when I was a child in the 1930s, for any child that had had an attack of tonsillitis to have their tonsils removed. This changed with the advent of penicillin in later years.

Once a week I gave anaesthetics for an ENT surgeon, Dr. Bob Lindsay, who made weekly visits to Cessnock Hospital from Newcastle. "Remove the tonsil, the whole tonsil and nothing but the tonsil' was his dictum. I watched him carefully dissect out the tonsils and tie off bleeding vessels when necessary. This gave me an advantage over the other junior doctors at Princess Margaret Hospital in Perth, when they were taught how to remove tonsils.

In Tara, Queensland, I did tonsillectomies on those needing it. Three patients with quinsy or recurrent tonsillitis in adults consulted me. No one before me had dared to operate as an adult tonsillectomy is a difficult operation due to scarring from repeated infections. However I was successful in removing 'the whole tonsils and nothing but the tonsils.'

Adult tonsillectomy is a painful procedure as the patients usually take a week or more to be able to swallow food. It was not so with the quinsy patients who said their pain was immediately better after the operation. They were swallowing almost anything within a few days post operation. They were very grateful.

4. MENINGOCOCCAL SEPTICAEMIA

When I was in Perth Children's Hospital, we had an epidemic of meningococcal septicaemia, which is a severe illness affecting the brain and nervous system and can cause blockage of blood vessels to the limbs, necessitating amputation. It is characterised by a severe fever with shivering and rigors, severe headaches, neck stiffness and a tell-tale petechial (spotty) rash. In small children the disease can spread rapidly, with death occurring within twelve hours or as early as five hours from the onset of the first symptoms, as in one case we had in Perth.

A small child aged nine months presented to me in Tara with a high fever and no localising signs. I gave the child some aspirin and told the mother I would be back in three or four hours after the morning surgery to re-examine. I had learned from paediatric training to examine babies about every 4 hours as things change rapidly compared with adults.

I received a phone call from the mother (a nurse) telling me not to bother coming as the rash had come out and he had measles.

"If he has measles, he is the only one within miles. I will come to check." I told her.

To my horror, the child had the classical meningococcal septicaemia rash and now a stiff neck. I very rapidly admitted the child to Tara's

107

small hospital and administered a large dose of penicillin. I did a lumbar puncture and proved the diagnosis, finding positive meningococci in the cerebral (brain) fluid. I delivered the appropriate treatment but thought I should check with Brisbane Children's' Hospital to see if I might have missed anything.

The paediatrician asked what condition the child was in, temperature, pulse, etc. "There is no need for you to transfer him. You have saved him."

We read about many disasters with this disease in recent times, and I cherished the valued experiences I gained in Perth Children's Hospital.

DISASTERS IN SURGERY

It doesn't take long after embarking on a career in surgery to realise that surgery is not totally free of complications or disasters.

I used to say to my junior staff, "There are five things that can happen when you operate on someone."

Firstly, you can get a perfect result. No matter how you tried you couldn't do better. This is what we strive for in each patient's operation and you get it every now and then.

Secondly, you can get a good result, an average success but maybe could have done a little better or better if you had attended to some minor part of the operation. This is the most usual result and the patients are very happy with the outcome.

Thirdly, you can operate and not improve things but not make the patient worse. Your operation may be difficult or have a low success rate and you may have warned the patient of this so that mostly they won't sue you.

Fourthly, you can operate and make the patient worse. You may have a large wound break down from infection or some other cause such that the patient is worse than before surgery. Every surgeon, even the best ones, gets a percentage of failures. You apologise and take extra care but realise a secondary or tertiary operation may be needed to achieve a satisfactory outcome. It is often best to refer the patient on to a reliable colleague as the patient may now have lost faith in their surgeon. Two eminent world famous rhinoplasty surgeons in Houston, Texas, U.S.A. cross-refer their failed cases. The patient is likely to sue you if you haven't adequately warned them of complications.

Fifthly, you can operate on the patient and have an unexpected post (or intra) operative death. This may be due to a pulmonary embolism or a coronary occlusion (heart attack), particularly in older, less fit patients. I have had at least four patients die from pulmonary embolisms or heart attacks, all unpredicted. I know of several patients who died of blood loss during surgery.

Nowadays patients can sue you for such. It is more distressing if the operation was not mandatory, as in cosmetic procedures.

I would tell my students, *until* after all five have happened to you on at least several occasions, you cannot consider yourself a trained or experienced surgeon

8 OVERSEAS CHARITABLE SURGERY TOURS

FIJI 1987

LABASA

The Australian Interplast Charity commenced sending plastic surgeons to the Pacific Region in 1983. The team, which consisted of two plastic surgeons, an anaesthetist and a trained theatre sister, first visited Apia, Samoa then West Timor. Besides the surgical team, there were unpaid extras such as wives and husbands and girlfriends. Interplast paid travel and accommodation as well as providing all necessary theatre and surgical equipment.

I was asked to go to Labasa (pronounced 'Lambasa') in July 1987 as this visit was not as popular as others were in the Pacific. Doris and plastic surgeon, John Newton, accompanied me. We did cleft lips and palates, burn scar contractures and hand injuries. A number of these were cut tendons in the hand caused by cane cutting injuries. We made a return visit in 1988 and on this occasion, I saw two patients who could not be treated locally because of the lack of specialist expertise. One was a teenage boy with an obstructive urinary passage who needed an expert children's urologist and the other was a child with a bent foot who needed osteotomies (a wedge of bone removed to straighten the foot) by an orthopaedic surgeon. I arranged for both to receive treatment in Newcastle.

An accompanying Rotarian, Barry Cooper from Bendigo in Victoria, took up the idea and sought funding for further patients in Fiji and other Pacific areas that needed specialist treatment in Australia. He founded a Rotary project called ROMAC - Rotary Overseas Medical Aid for Children. The organisation grew and now has treated over fifteen hundred patients and has over one hundred patients on the waiting list. One set of Siamese twins achieved much T.V. and press attention.

Of my 41 trips to the developing world, more than half were to the Pacific Island countries.

This man from Kiribati, in the photo opposite, had two school-aged children who did the shopping, as he would not go out. After surgery he was able to socialise.

In 1989, Fiji had a general election in which the local Indian population (brought to Fiji as cane cutters and now numbering more than 50% of the population) won the majority in the election. Colonel Rambucca, a local Fijian, decided that the migrant Indians were not fit to govern Fiji and staged a coup d'état. He rewrote the constitution ensuring that the Parliament had over 50% native Fijians in control. Rambucca introduced mandatory Sunday religious observance. The new

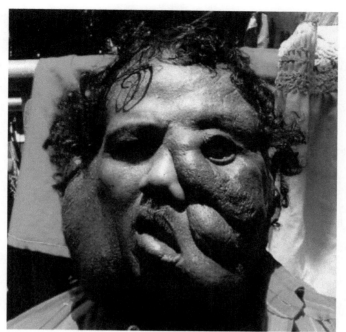

Neurofibroma face "Elephant Man", Kiribati, 2005

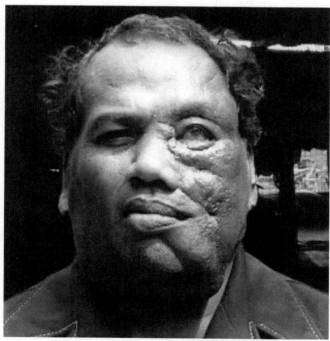

"Elephant Man" one month post operation

Government also came down on Indians in high positions that also included doctors, resulting in Indian doctors leaving to find jobs in Australia, New Zealand and other countries. Nearly half of all medical personnel departed. Interplast abandoned its visits until the politics settled some years later.

AFRICA

MALAWI AND MOZAMBIQUE

I had a phone call from a Rotarian friend, Kevin Leary of Toronto Club, asking me to go to Malawi, Africa, to do some plastic surgery. This fitted in well in 1989 now that Fiji was off the agenda. He told me he was going to build a handicap centre in Blantyre, a two-year Rotary project. I asked if he would see who was doing the plastic surgery and whether there was a need for my particular expertise.

Two weeks after his arrival, he phoned from Malawi saying that a Canadian surgeon had been there for five years but had returned to Canada three years ago and now there was no plastic surgeon for a population of ten million people. At the time, Australia had two hundred plastic surgeons for twenty million people - a somewhat different ratio!

I contacted the Canadian doctor who gave me some excellent advice. She said that if you think of something you need and can't do without, take it, as what they have will be missing or broken. *How right she was!*

I took a case full of instruments, suture material, dressings, etc. I found they were re-using skin graft knife blades (3) and re-sharpening them. Have you ever tried re-using a shaving blade? They were hopelessly inadequate. The first time I took a skin graft with a new blade, the staff commented, "That was so easy." Of course, it would be with the right equipment. Fine suture material for clefts was absent and dressing materials in short supply. We did lots of burn contractures, cleft lips and palates and other traumatic injuries. I took large quantities of surgical gloves and noted they were washing disposable gloves and re-using them.

I made yearly visits to Malawi which included two areas, Blantyre and Lilongwe (the airport centre), spending six weeks with each visit. My trips were organised by Dr. Michael King.

The Dean of the Faculty of Medicine at Newcastle University, a Professor Mac... phoned to tell me he had a doctor from Mozambique who wanted to speak to a plastic/burns surgeon.

A meeting was arranged with Riccardo Barradas, surgeon, who was in Newcastle learning how to run a medical school. He had one year's training in burn surgery in the U.K. He spoke perfect English (Portugese is the lingua franca in Mozambique). We agreed to my adding two weeks on my next Malawi visit to work in Mozambique.

We treated burn contractures and some new burns but little else. The local E.N.T. surgeon was treating all the clefts and did not want any help. Sadly, he was using an outdated cleft lip repair technique.

Mozambique, a former Portuguese colony received independence in the early 1960s. The Renamo rebels were (and still are) an opposition political group who virtually wrecked the country. They blew up the bridges so you couldn't use the beautiful highways. The country's main industry, cashew nuts, could not be harvested. As a result Mozambique became one of the poorest countries in Africa. Maputo, the capital was an island city where one could not go more than twenty-five kilometres outside without getting shot by rebel forces. One lawyer drove outside late at night and was caught and shot by the rebels. A couple tried to cross into Tanzania at one o'clock in the morning, a fifty-kilometre journey. The rebels caught them, took all their possessions and they returned to Mozambique naked.

"You were lucky you weren't killed," the locals told me.

The Renamo Rebels brutalised the population and we saw patients who had parts of their bodies cut off. If you can think of something that can be cut off, they did it. Hands, noses ears, feet, breasts and genitals. I saw one seventeen-year-old lad who was emasculated by the rebels and I have never seen a sadder face. You can reconstruct a penis and testicles but never make the patient sexually functional. Fortunately, the perpetrators of this act were caught and shot.

The rebels would demand a teenage boy shoot his parents dead otherwise, they would throw him onto a fire to be burnt to death. In this way, they recruited child soldiers. There were many other atrocities perpetrated by the rebels too hideous to mention.

Nearly two million refugees from Mozambique moved into Malawi to avoid the civil war. International aid funded their housing in camps along the border.

The Jehovah's' Witness community refused blood transfusions and the brotherhood act of sharing cut fingers and so avoided sharing blood. As a result and together with a moral lifestyle, there was a lower incidence of HIV infection and AIDS in their community!

The United Nations held an internationally supervised election in which the local government won and the Renamo Rebels became the opposition party, which they accepted as a paid job and the civil war ended. United Nations officials spent two or three years organising the elections resulting in a rise in the economy although food was dearer. After the elections, investment in the country re-started and Mozambique thrived once more. I noted a sudden increase in the number of Mercedes taxis available.

There were about two thousand orphaned street kids in the capital, Maputo. They would ask to mind your parked car for a few shillings; you accepted this otherwise you would find your tyres let down. About fifty kids were sleeping under awnings at the local Catholic convent. This was the overflow with another one hundred and fifty inside. The nuns taught them to read and write so they could get a job and not become thieves and beggars. I gave the convent all my spare money on departure.

My invitations to Mozambique ceased when my contact, Dr. Riccardo Baradas left the hospital service. I became more occupied with American groups.

All of my trips to Africa, accompanied by Doris, were self-funded. Doris estimated they cost me $25,000 each visit in lost earnings. However, they were wonderful and worthwhile experiences.

UGANDA

Medical people in Africa came to know of my African trips and I received a request from the Dean of the Medical Faculty of Uganda's university, centred at Makere Hospital in Kampala, Uganda. I agreed to visit and spent an additional two weeks tacked on to my Malawi visits. The yearly salary offered by the Dean was equal to the amount I could earn in two weeks in my private practise in Australia.

He told me, "Obviously you would need to do some private work to earn a living."

I turned down the offer of a two-year stint as Director of Plastic Surgery and made visits each year.

For many years, Uganda had been under the control of President Idi Amin who had left three years before my visit.

The country was very run down with unrepaired roads and so on. Idi Amin was called "the butcher of Africa". He would drive around in his bulletproof car with his motorcade. If anyone crossed in front of him he would have them caught and shot. There were many stories of his barbarity. He invited his newly formed parliamentary members to a house party.

He asked what they liked to drink. "Whisky? Here is a case for you. Wine?"

He then opened a large refrigerator in which were the severed heads of his rivals and he told the parliamentarians, "This is what happens to those who challenge my authority! You have to go out and get your own salaries by similar means of extortion!"

President Obote succeded Amin and he wasn't much better. The UN came in to hold elections.

The Ugandan Malago Hospital was very run down with repairs needed everywhere. There was always a shortage of nursing staff.

On one of my first operating sessions, I asked for some small scissors for a small child's cleft repair. They gave me a pair with the tip broken off on one side, which were useless. I asked for another pair and was given a twelve-inch pair, far too big for a small child! Fortunately Doris had some fine, small iris scissors in her hand bag which I used for the removal of sutures and these saved the day.

There are six operating theatres in Malago Hospital and my allocated theatre was full of blowflies. I killed them off with insect spray and investigated the other five theatres. Sure enough, they were also full of blowflies. The other surgeons seemed oblivious to the flies as being part of living in Africa. Further investigation revealed a large open door, which I immediately closed thus reducing the influx of flies.

I operated on a bilateral cleft lip and palate with a fairly good result.

The mother said, "A million, million thanks Doctor. No-one could have done it better."

Her comments were worth more than money to me. She was an intelligent and educated person who spoke all eight local languages. She did the rounds with me acting as interpreter.

Those in charge never turned patients away from the hospital. Extra patients slept between or under the beds. There was no 'McDonald House' and relatives slept out in the open yards surrounding the hospital. They certainly couldn't afford motels like in this country.

We spent much time teaching surgical techniques to local surgeons. One American group of anaesthetists were teaching non-medical technicians how to give anaesthetics. I was told there had been four avoidable anaesthetic deaths due to the learning process.

When Mulago Hospital was refurbishing its theatres, I was told to stay away as there would be emergency surgery only. For some reason, they did not invite me back.

FATUMA NANGOBI

Fatuma Nangobi was a Ugandan African child aged about seven years when I first met her. She had suffered burns to her body, face, and had developed a severe keloid scarring of the right ear. This needed excision of the keloid and grafting followed by radiotherapy to prevent keloid recurrence together with silicon pressure moulds to cover the scars, also serving to lessen keloid recurrence. This could not be done in Uganda as they had no Radiotherapy at that time.

I was attending a European plastic surgery meeting when a Professor X from Nigeria gave a talk on treating keloid scars in Africa. I spoke to him afterwards and told him of this Ugandan girl who needed specialised treatment including radiotherapy and would he be able to do it.

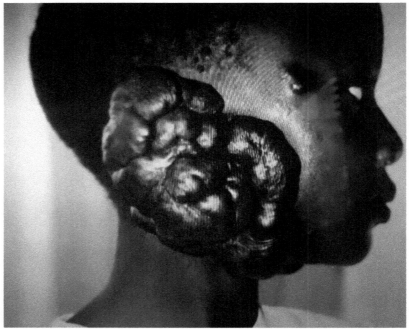

Fatuma Nangobi Keloid scar, right ear

"Of course, send me her photo and I will take her on."

I forwarded the photos only to receive a reply that the case was too difficult to treat and he was opting out. Quite possibly, he wasn't prepared to do it without payment.

Nonsense! I thought. *I will treat her in Newcastle, Australia, myself.*

With the help of Rotary and others in Uganda, the government paid expenses for her and her mother to come to Australia for treatment.

She arrived with her mother and a small suitcase between the two of them. By then, she was aged about nine or ten years. I arranged for and treated her keloid at Lake Macquarie Private Hospital, all at no charge. The keloid was treated together with release of other scar contractures and all went well. Her radiotherapy was also done at no cost, as were silicon moulds for her ear, which she wore for three months.

A television company (I think NBN) did a documentary on her story.

She left Australia after three months with her mother and 100kgs of luggage, which was well over weight allowance. Qantas, having viewed the documentary, allowed the excess at no cost.

Matron Scott of Lake Macquarie Private Hospital offered to pay Fatuma's school fees for her education and was given the headmaster's contact details. She forwarded the money only for each term's education. After one year, she received a letter from Fatuma asking when the money was coming. It seems the headmaster was pocketing the lot! Typical of Africa, I thought.

Some years later, Matron Scott received a letter from Fatuma Nangobi's sister saying she had found the address in past mail from Matron. Fatuma had died at age twenty-two. Apparently, she developed a pain in the stomach with vomiting and died a few days later never having seen a doctor. As a surgeon, I would say that there was almost a one hundred percent chance that whatever was wrong with her could have been cured by surgery at her age.

I was sad that all our good work had been for almost nothing. Such is Africa!

GHANA

While I was at a surgical meeting of the European Plastic Surgery Section in Turkey, I met one of my old bosses, 'Jake' Mustardee from Ayrshire, Scotland. He said he was looking for an Australian plastic surgeon who was working in Africa.

"You mean me?"

He had set up a plastic surgery unit in Accra, Ghana, with funding from the UK and a monthly visit there by UK plastic surgeons. I agreed to do one month's surgery and extended this to six weeks as the following surgeon had cancelled his visit.

Accompanied by Doris, we arrived at Accra airport to find nobody there to meet us. I had trouble with the local Africans always wanting to carry our bags for a fee. I didn't have the address of our stay except that is was a 'Shell Guesthouse'. Eventually we were taken to the Shell manager's house and he directed us to the guesthouse. On arrival at 11pm the occupants informed us we were expected tomorrow. Fortunately, I had become African wise and I knew how to handle the situation.

The traffic in Accra was chronically congested. A military driver who drove in a madly aggressive manner taking chances and forcing his wrong or right of way, took us to and from the hospital. Initially I travelled in the front passenger seat but soon moved to the safer back seat. After some weeks, the military driver inevitably had a road accident and he was in the wrong. He was sacked as our driver. At almost every set of traffic lights there were long delays with hawkers at the roadside trying to sell you anything.

My contact surgeon, a Dr. Paintsel, was an excellent technician and spoke all the local languages. I gave him a two-hour lecture on plastic surgery each day for five weeks. We treated lots of fresh burns as well as clefts, injuries and head and neck cancers. They were changing the dressings on the leg donor site every few days causing much pain to the patient. I introduced a plastic cover over the tulle on the donor site that could be left intact for two or three weeks. This resulted in no pain and good healing.

We saw several cases of Burkit's Lymphoma which is a large facial tumour caused by a virus. It can be cured satisfactorily with chemotherapy. One patient with a large tumour had had a biopsy taken the day before I arrived. The pathology result never came through and some weeks later I told my assistant to get the oncology department to go ahead and treat the patient without the pathology report. Sadly, he had no treatment whilst I was in Ghana. Such is the speed of things there!

Before leaving Ghana, I went to a meeting of the East African Surgical Association and there gave a lecture on flap repairs of compound fractures of the leg and other skin defects. A surgeon from Rwanda approached me and told me that following the war, he had fifty-seven patients that I could treat. Unfortunately, I couldn't spare the time to go there. There is a great lack of expertise in Africa.

I did no further work in Ghana as the Scottish organisation found it cost twice as much to fund my airfares compared to visits by UK surgeons. My African visits ceased for one or other reasons and I became more involved with trips organised by the American groups, 'Rotaplast' and 'Alliance for Smiles".

POVERTY AND THEFT IN THE DEVELOPING WORLD

In many of the countries I have visited poverty is extreme, such that the so-called 'poverty line' in Australia would apply to over ninety percent of the population. This results in theft sometimes by organised gangs but always petty theft and pickpockets.

Johannesburg was voted the most violent city in the world on the basis of its violent attacks and death rate per head of the population. There could be as many as fifty attacks per night.

I met an orthopaedic surgeon in Uganda who had been working there for seven years teaching the locals. He had a large house with a high fence to keep out intruders. As was the custom, on arriving home at night, you beeped on the horn of your car and the servants would open your gates. He arrived home one night around eleven o'clock and was met by a group of criminals who shot him dead and stole his 4WD Toyota car.

A plastic surgeon in Johannesburg was driving home in his BMW late one night and was ambushed and shot dead for his car.

Almost everyone in Jo'burg can tell you of some friend or relative who was murdered for theft of possessions and or money. Car theft was particularly common such that BMW designed a car that spurted out flames if anybody nearby tried to enter the car without deactivating the security system.

I met a friend who owned a Volkswagen Combi Van. These could be easily stolen by breaking into the front driver's door and disconnecting the battery to disable the security system and hot-wiring the ignition. My friend was an auto electrician and had put a system in place such that whenever the battery was reconnected a loud hooting alarm was activated, so you couldn't drive it away. That system worked beautifully!

I went to a plastic surgery meeting in Rio De Janeiro, Brazil in the early eighties. Doris and I stayed at the Sheraton Hotel in a beach area. I used to go swimming and jogging along the four hundred metre beach each morning. One day I found all my clothes gone. The next day I had Doris mind them and she saw a group of youths come down the stairs at one end of the beach and walk in file, combing the beach for anything worth stealing, leaving by the stairs at the other end. I had thought the beach private for the exclusive use of the hotel. It was not so.

A notice at the entrance to the beach from the hotel read 'ANY TOWELS NOT RETURNED MUST BE PAID FOR.' Perhaps it should have read, 'THIS IS A PUBLIC BEACH. DO NOT LEAVE ANY PROPERTY UNATTENDED.'

I returned to our room wearing only my swimming costume and received some interesting looks as I made my way in the lift.

I like classical music and decided to go to a concert in an outer suburb of Rio. I enquired at the front desk of the hotel. The receptionist advised me, "Do not go there. They will see you are a gringo and they will rob you!" Wisely, I didn't go.

A plastic surgeon colleague went for a swim at the famous Copacabana Beach. His wife was sunning on the beach with his watch and hotel keys wrapped in a towel behind her head and she held a camera on her abdomen in front. A youth jumped on her stomach and stole the camera. She chased him and got it back, however others stole the towel and its contents.

Doris left her reading glasses in a restaurant. She went back for them only minutes later to discover they were gone!

Papua New Guinea is known to be a tough place with many 'rascals' (impoverished out of work itinerants) roaming the streets. I was told, "Carry a ten Kina note (about AU$5) in your pocket and offer it to them if challenged. They are usually after money for food."

A Rotarian President of Port Moresby Rotary Club used to travel from work by car only two blocks to the Rotary Meetings as she had been accosted so many times when walking just that short distance!

Local Rotarians invited me to dinner and picked me up in a 4WD car. I knew there were ambushes along the roads in PNG and asked my acquaintance, "Do you have any trouble with rascals ambushing you?"

He replied, "Oh no, I can drive off the road and avoid the ambush. I know where they are most of the time and I carry this gun (pulling out a large heavy handgun)."

"Have you ever shot anyone with that?" I asked.

"Yes, twelve!"

In Port Moresby Hospital, I saw a patient who had been shot in the chest with a bow and arrow. That is something you don't see in Australia.

At the distant perimeter of the golf course a security guard stood carrying a bow and arrows.

In Mozambique, my contact person, Dr. Riccardo Barradas told me, that if you are approached by a policeman who takes your camera on some pretext, offer him US$5 to give it back for that's all he could sell it for.

It was easy to park your car in Maputo, Mozambique as the sixteen-year civil war had left the country economically destitute with four thousand orphan street kids. A small boy would ask you, "Can I mind your car for you Sir?" He would collect about twenty cents on your return. You always agreed to the offer because if you didn't you could be sure your tyres would all be let down. Theft of windscreen wipers was also common but you could go to a market and buy them back.

If we went anywhere there was a crowd, Riccardo would warn, "Watch your pocket." I always kept my hand on my wallet and this prevented any pickpocketing.

I met a lady specialist radiologist who was doing a six month tour of duty at the major hospital in Maputo. She told me she had been mugged three times whilst walking in the town streets. She would be knocked over from behind and her bag stolen. The muggings stopped only when she dressed like a local person, wearing jeans, no dress, no purse, no watch and no jewellery.

I enjoyed taking photos of interesting subjects like a burnt out car, a post box no longer in use and so on. To avoid being mugged I hid my camera under a towel in a plastic bag. Everyone carried their goods in a plastic bag and no-one robbed them. I would take my camera out when no one was looking to capture my photos.

I stayed in borrowed accommodation in a flat in Maputo and parked my borrowed car on the wide road median strip. On leaving my car one day, a street kid offered me a cigarette lighter for sale. Being a non-smoker, I said no. The price went down such that by the time I reached my front door, it was one third of the original asking price.

I gave the boy a note worth about one dollar Australian. On inspection of the cigarette lighter, I could see it was second hand and had been opened, refilled with lighter fluid and glued shut. I realised I had bought about five millilitres of lighter fluid worth about five cents. Such was the enterprise of the starving orphan kids of Mozambique.

Maputo had United Nations personnel come in to organise elections, which took about two and a half years. One UN lady asked me to take her home after dinner as there had been five murders in the street where we were going. As we went by a group of youths sleeping under cardboard asked us in Portuguese for money for food.

"We haven't any money," she told them. They always say it is for food but it's often for cigarettes. I had to go back the same way and didn't get mugged!

When we returned home to Australia after trips overseas to poor countries, Doris would say, "Let's kiss the ground!" She felt very appreciative of the country in which we live.

AFRICAN INDEPENDENCE

When Nelson Mandela, leader of the ANC political party, was freed from gaol after twenty-three years confined to Robben Island, he was elected president and was leader of the ANC political party.

During Apartheid it was a rule that you had to have an identification card and you weren't allowed to travel from city to city without government authorization. Nelson Mandela abolished the cards and as a result, there was an influx of Africans from all over South Africa such that around two million migrants arrived in Johannesburg, two million in Durban and one million in Cape Town. Many Africans looking for a better life left their bankrupt countries where often the unemployment rate was as high as fifty percent. With so many in South Africa, they had to live by begging or stealing with organised crime.

I stayed in a hotel in Cape Town and there was a large market place on the waterfront about a mile away across vacant land. I told the hotel I was going to walk to the market. They said I must take a taxi as people are mugged or murdered walking across there. I took a taxi! I asked the taxi driver if he had had any trouble with the local criminals.

"Yes. I had just started work at six o'clock one morning when youths hailed my cab. They got in and demanded money. I gave then fifteen rand, which was all I had for change. They said I had more and was hiding it somewhere. Because I didn't have any other money they smashed all my windows and left," he told me.

It is a sad fact that, having achieved independence, the economies of most African countries have gone down under black rule with gross mismanagement and corruption. This has also resulted in an exodus of doctors and other professionals from these countries. There are more Malawian doctors in Canada than in Malawi.

Zimbabwe is another classic example with the economy running at thirty percent after Mugabe took over.

ROTAPLAST - PERU AND CHINA

My theatre sister, Lyn Thorpe, was invited to Peru by another sister who had organised some surgery to be done by a Newcastle paediatric surgeon. The trip was badly organised and not much useful surgery was done. However Lyn met Rotaplast's main contact in Lima, Peru. She told him about my work elsewhere and I was invited to join Rotaplast, which is an American plastic surgery group centred in San Francisco.

The Rotaplast teams consist of three or four surgical groups each of about eight people, a plastic surgeon, an anaesthetist and other assistants. These, plus extras, amounted to a group of thirty or forty people as well as a truckload of medical gear.

Our first trip was to La Oroya, Peru, in the Andes. It is a smelly mining town twelve thousand feet up in the mountains, with polluted air from the smelters. I took maximum protection against altitude sickness, as we would go straight there in day one with no opportunity to acclimatise. I suffered no altitude sickness.

One severe bilateral lip patient was seen by the other two surgeons in the group who said they couldn't do it in one operation and needed staged procedures. I offered to do it in one stage and they willingly passed the patient over to me. Many congratulations came my way when I was successfully able to repair lip and palate with a good outcome for the patient.

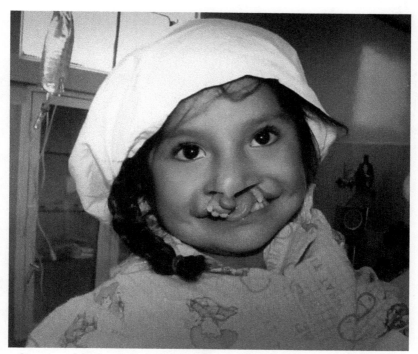

Severe bilateral cleft lip and palate, La Oroya, Peru, 2004

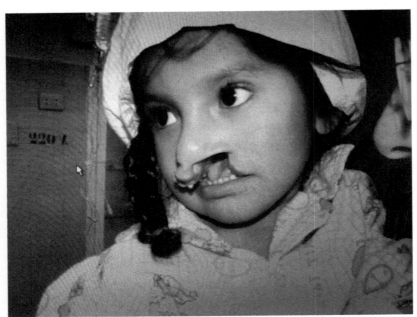

Lateral view

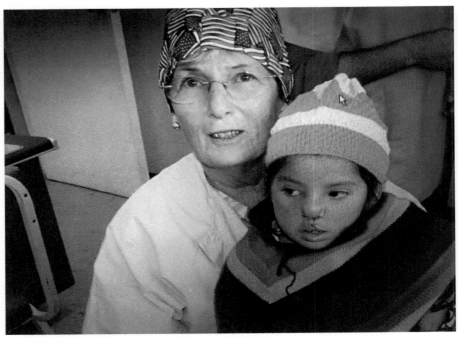

Lyn and child with repaired bilateral cleft, La Oroya,
Peru, 2004

We worked all day from 7.00 am to 7.00 pm doing predominantly cleft surgery. We recorded our operations and assessed their costs in US dollars. I completed over US$100,000 worth of surgery in around thirty operations, some of which were combined lip and palate.

One Chinese American surgeon, Wally Chang, was a Director of Alliance for Smiles (AFS), which was a breakaway group from Rotaplast and run on the same lines. They had set up to do extra work in China, which Rotaplast would not do. Wally invited me to join AFS and I went on my first trip to Wenzhou, China in about 2006. This was followed by trips to Harbin, and one later to Wenzhou again. Alliance for Smiles made some attempts to teach other surgeons which Rotaplast sadly did not.

In China with the one child policy, we saw a lot of patients for minor revisions of cleft lips, as the parents wanted a perfect looking child, often a girl. On one female child, I did a revision involving two small scars on the upper lip with a near perfect, virtually undetectable result. The mother was so overjoyed she wrote me a two page letter of thanks.

With a two year break between my visits to Wenzhou, China's growing economy was such that the number of pedal-operated rickshaw taxis was reduced by two thirds and the number of expensive cars increased three fold.

ROTAPLAST AND OPS IN THE PACIFIC REGION

As we found travelling to South America took us two days each way, we asked for jobs in the Pacific region as an alternative. I made two visits to the Philippines with an Australian group called PAMA (Philippine Australia Medical Association).

Our first trips were to Bago City (2008) and Cebu (2009) in the Philippines. In Cebu we were accommodated in a motel in the heart of the city. We visited Cebu's guitar and stringed instrument factory with some of the most expensive guitars in the world made and sold there. With my love of music, I was tempted to buy a beautiful mandolin but desisted.

We visited several smaller islands, and at times, operating conditions were primitive. Consequently we had to modify our surgery, avoiding cases which were too complicated.

In one village all boys aged about five to seven years were traditionally circumcised by local GPs. This amounted to a 'dorsal slit' and not a full circumcision with removal of the whole foreskin. Re-education of the local GPs was needed. I ceased visits with PAMA due to other commitments

OSSA (Overseas Surgical Service Australia)

I had one trip with OSSA to West Timor in 2007. Local officials screened us heavily before we went up to Haliluluk to work. They wanted to know if we were competent to operate on their people (with no rewards !?!).

We drove for five hours to reach the Catholic Mission hospital (150 beds) at Haliluluk. I did twenty-eight clefts and on the last day ran out of suture material. At a presentation dinner, I was asked to speak without notice and said something like this:

"Thank you for inviting us to operate in your hospital. With God's help and the assistance of your dedicated medical staff we have made a great difference to the lives of the twenty-eight people operated on and I thank you immensely."

They didn't ask me what religion I was and I didn't offer to tell them. Christian compassion is the same in all religions no matter what brand.

The chief plastic surgeon organiser, perhaps due to professional jealousy, didn't offer to have me on another visit to West Timor.

Rotaplast invited me to go to Nagamangala, India, a university hospital some five hours north of Bangalore. We treated mainly clefts and burns, some old, some recent. A visiting surgeon was able to do follow-up consultations with our post-operation patients.

Further surgical missions with Rotaplast were to Sylhet and Dhaka, Bangladesh, in 2014 with my last visit to Dhaka taking place in February 2015.

Most of my surgical sponsors decided that at over eighty, I was too old to take on more surgery in spite of the fact that I have excellent health and surgical skills. On my last trip the other two surgeons rated me the best of the three. Certainly, I have more experience after forty-one trips. In some ways, I was happy to leave behind twelve-hour operating days at eighty-six years of age.

9 "RETIREMENT"

MY MEDICO-LEGAL PRACTICE

I retired on my birthday 14th May 1994 at sixty-five and ceased medical practice in Newcastle, taking a four months overseas holiday. I sold my rooms to a local ophthalmologist.

With Doris, I spent four and a half months holidaying overseas. We visited the U.K., Canada and the USA followed by three months in Africa doing surgery in the four countries visited: Malawi, Mozambique, Uganda and Ghana. I reckoned on spending all my superannuation until age seventy-five when I would go on the aged pension. At age seventy-five, I extended this to age eighty-fives and again extended it to eighty-nine.

In October 1998, I received a telephone call from the director of a medical insurance company IMO - Independent Medical Opinions. Ms. Brough said she had viewed my C.V. and found I had the experience and qualifications that her company could use and was thus invited to join the company to do medico-legal work.

I started doing half a day (a maximum of five consultations) every two weeks. This soon built up and other companies made similar offers. Within one and a half years, I found myself doing one to one and a half days each week on medical insurance work. Other companies were M.S.B.C. (Medical Specialists Booking Service), Medlaw, S.O.G. (Specialist Opinion Group), A.M.L.G. (Australian Medico Legal Group), Sinergy and E-Reports. The amount of work varied from a full session of four to five consultations once a week to occasional assessments once a month. In this mix were also private consultations in Newcastle only, mostly from local legal firms. I attended all training sessions and became fully qualified to assess upper limb, facial injuries, skin and scars (many burns) and medical negligence cases. The predominant injury assessment was of hand, wrist and arm injuries followed by skin injuries (burns and traumatic scars).

Patients would often come scared of the surgeon but I had several techniques for putting them at ease and I felt I was generally a user-friendly doctor as opposed to some who were more aloof and unfriendly.

One patient was particularly talkative. I waited until she ran out of words.

"Doctor, you actually listened to me!" she remarked. "The last specialist stopped me talking saying, 'Shut up, I'll ask the questions, You just answer them!"

The majority of patients were not trying to abuse the system and would get back to work as soon as possible. But some, particularly where a legal firm was involved, would stretch out their injury to a maximum.

For example, a self-employed person with a single finger injury would be off work for no more than a few days or a week or two at most. A compensation cheat would be off for two years with the same injury and all efforts to get them back to work would fail!

Medical negligence cases were increasing at an exponential rate. When I started practice as a plastic surgeon in 1968, I paid $75 per year for medical legal insurance. When I retired in 1995, I was paying $15,000 per year and thought this a bit much. It is now $80,000 a year and rising. The legal profession say they don't know a thing about medicine but they do know *how to sue*!

The obstetricians have been badly treated. There is at least a 1-2% or more chance of an unfavourable outcome with any birth. (A horse stud master will tell you it's fifteen to twenty percent with horses.) In spite of all preventive measures and full advice, obstetricians get sued out of business after ten or more years of obstetric practice when their insurance premiums reach a level making it no longer possible to practise - generally when they are at their peak of expertise.

In Tara in Western Queensland over three and a half years, I supervised sixty-five births a year, handling all complications with good results. It is now almost impossible for me, or any general practitioner without an obstetrics degree, to practise in a remote area.

MEDICAL NEGLIGENCE CASES

I was sent a number of medical negligence cases for assessment. In quite a number of cases, the patient had a legitimate cause for suing.

One "cowboy" surgeon, a general surgeon with no training in plastic or cosmetic surgery, used to arrive from Melbourne at a Sydney private hospital on a Thursday morning, operating during the day, and go home to Melbourne on Thursday night leaving his patients in the care of a G.P. with a surgical degree but no training in cosmetic surgery. He did an abdominoplasty (tummy tuck) on a morbidly obese woman who really needed weight reduction or bariatric (weight reduction) surgery. He did a brief post operation review and went home as usual on Thursday night. The patient was in pain with a large haematoma (blood collection) below the abdominal flap. She was seen the next day by the G.P. surgeon who failed to recognise this major complication and authorised her discharge the following day (now Saturday). She had so much pain she returned to hospital the following day (Sunday) and was seen by the hospital administrator, a non-nurse or medically trained person who told her everything was okay.

She consulted her G.P. on Monday because of ongoing symptoms and was told he could do nothing and to return to her surgical advisors. The wound broke down exuding a large amount of blood clot and fluid. She was re-admitted to hospital and seen by her original operating surgeon on his next operating Thursday. Quite wrongly, he attempted to repair the wound with large tension sutures. Again, he left to return to Melbourne. A day or two later the wound inevitably broke down again leaving a gaping hole. She was then seen by her G.P. who quite sensibly referred her to a competent plastic surgeon The plastic surgeon repaired the wound correctly with a skin graft followed by ten days hospitalisation.

She asked me if she had a case for negligence against the original surgeon.

"You can't lose." I told her.

"But tell me how much you get in settlement."

It was $800,000.

There were a number of other cases of 'gung ho', incompetent, untrained surgeons doing operations they were not capable of doing with consequent disastrous results.

On the other hand, I encountered a number of patients who would sue the surgeon for no good reason, such as a scar, which might be thickened, a minor imbalance of breasts and so on.

One lady had a reduction mammoplasty (breast reduction) operation, her third cosmetic procedure, and was suing the doctor because he didn't reduce the size enough. He said she would fit into a "B" cup bra, but could only manage a "C" cup. Examination revealed quite a nice result from what were obviously large breasts. The lawyer asked me to phone him with my opinion.

"Have you a pre-operation photo of the patient's breasts?" I asked.

"No." He replied.

"Well, I can tell you her surgeon will certainly have one, which is a routine pre-op procedure. You are going to look silly in court if the pre and post op photos are shown and all you are suing for is an error of bra size assessment by the surgeon who has produced a good result." Personally, I never gave patients a bra size assessment just telling them I would reduce as much as reasonably possible. The lawyer advised his client not to sue.

Lawyers advised patients in many other cases to drop their complaints because there was no good reason to sue. A common one was thickened scars. Patients vary in their scar forming ability, some with fine scars, others with thick keloid scars as wide as half a centimetre. My practice was always to draw the scars on a drawing of the operation indicating the possibility of the development of a thick keloid and showing the size of that possible keloid.

I have never been sued in the whole of my medical and surgical career, which I believe is due to my attitude to patients. I could have been sued on a number of occasions but wasn't. Why?

This is what I think made the difference:

Be nice to people. Don't be overbearing or adopt a higher than you attitude. Always listen and hear them out. Adopt techniques that put them at ease.

Don't offer to do cosmetic surgery that they don't ask for and don't do any operation you wouldn't recommend for yourself or your family.

Always inform the patient of complications e.g. thick scars, asymmetry, and the possible need to do secondary surgery.

Keep accurate records.

Don't do any operation you are not trained to do. Draw diagrams for the patient.

List complications in your notes as these are likely to be read by their lawyer.

Nowadays patients are given an operation information sheet listing everything and a computer program has been devised which ensures the client has understood the risks.

If things do go wrong? Admit the error at once to the patient and say *Sorry*. Be ultra-attentive and do more than usual post op visits. Refer the patient on to a competent colleague for ongoing treatment before they change doctors themselves, having lost confidence in you.

I have had two cases where the patient was going to sue me but the lawyer found they had no case.

Every surgeon gets disasters. I had a patient having a breast reconstruction with a Tram (trans abdominal myocutaneous Flap). The breast reconstruction was OK but the abdominal wound broke down due to infection leaving a large gaping hole. The best management is to allow the wound to heal with dressing over two months and revise the scar later.

The patient who was a nurse said she was going to a proper surgeon in Sydney for further treatment I suggested she ask him if he had ever had a major wound breakdown like this. If he said "No" then you are dealing with a liar or a very inexperienced surgeon. I warned her that attempts to repair the wound would fail. I never saw the end result.

I did a breast reduction with quite a satisfactory primary result. Unfortunately, the patient was allergic to the absorbable suture material and all wounds broke down. I passed the patient on to a colleague who managed the patient through to a satisfactory outcome and she could breast feed.

If you are nice to patients, they will be more likely to think you couldn't have made a mistake and it must have been something in them. Surgery is not a trouble free art and one has to reckon on this knowledge.

10 My Relationships

DORIS

I met Sister Doris Hyams in 1954 when I was a new graduate. I was being shown over the Cessnock hospital when we first saw each other and she told herself that she was going to marry me. Doris was just twenty-two years old and I was twenty-four.

After a whirlwind romance, we were married in the registry office on the 1st July, 1954. Doris was a Christadelphian and I was not, so we couldn't marry in her church. We lived in the Cessnock hospital quarters while I worked there.

Doris had our first child at St John of God Maternity Hospital and we named her Alison Lee Walker. As reported earlier, Alison had renal abnormalities, which eventually led to her death at thirteen. The loss of Alison hit us both hard.

Doris gave birth to two more children, Colin on 10th April 1959 and David on 24rd November 1960, both born at Toowoomba Hospital under Dr. Harbison. At the time, I was Medical Superintendent of the Tara hospital and in private practice at the same time.

Doris was pregnant in 1962 when we moved to the UK with the three children. During her pregnancy, she developed gestational diabetes and, at thirty-six weeks, the foetus died.

The diabetes she developed in 1963 continued to dog Doris for the rest of her life. It took the lives of our twins, who died at birth in Manchester and, following our return to Australia in 1968, a little girl who died of respiratory failure twenty-two hours post-delivery.

Doris was put on long acting and short acting insulin. She would have frequent hypoglycaemic (low blood sugar) attacks and I would treat these by giving her oral sugar in the form of sweets or sweet drinks. I administered intravenous glucose when she was too deeply comatosed to swallow. We had vials of 20% glucose with 10 ml syringes in her purse and everywhere else. I became an expert in early detection and treatment of her low sugar episodes. On long car journeys, she would be my relief driver with some interesting results. I knew she was "hypo" by her lack of sense of speed and direction and so would grab the wheel and shout, "Pull over!" to get her to stop for treatment!

I resuscitated Doris literally hundreds of times and about five times when she was in a deep hypoglycaemic coma, which could have caused death or brain damage.

OUR FIGHT FOR DORIS'S LIFE

As the years passed, Doris' diabetes began to catch up with her and she developed a degree of heart failure, renal failure and loss of vision. She had bilateral cataract extractions with silicon lens replacements. She had many laser treatments to the vessels at the back of the eyes to prevent catastrophic bleeding and blindness. Her ophthalmic surgeon did an excellent job on her eyes such that she was still able to read until a month before her final illness. She became less and less able to walk and used a walking frame for mobility. We couldn't go anywhere that had stairs and we made much use of disability car parking spaces. By then she was on maximal treatment for heart failure and diabetes.

DORIS'S DEATH

"One of these days you will get an infection and your weakened body system will be unable to cope." I told her.

I returned from an overseas trip to the Philippines with an URTI (cold plus flu) which Doris contracted from me. She developed pneumonia and was unfit to do anything. She was admitted to Shortland Masonic Hospital (a rehab unit for older people) under the care of a geriatrician, Dr. Wallace. It was the 15th December 2009 and three days before her 78th birthday on the 18th. Her condition slowly deteriorated. Her diabetic physician, Dr. Jack Fowler had retired and left her to a young endocrinologist Dr. X who took three months off to have a baby and didn't get to see Doris until 10th January 2010.

Dr. X changed Doris' insulin to a newer (better?) brand and this caused her to have more "hypos" (low blood sugar episodes) than usual. Her exercise tolerance had lessened to a point where she could hardly walk twenty yards along the hospital corridor. In the very early hours of Sunday 24th January 2010, she had an unrecognised hypo and the nurses found her dead early next morning. We knew she was not recovering so her death was not unexpected.

Doris' death was the most devastating thing that had ever happened to me after fifty-four and a half years of very happy marriage. Recovery would take a long time.

About 180 people turned up for her funeral and I received multiple letters of condolence. One lady told me she always remembered how kind Doris was when seeing my patients in and out. That lady's visit had been more than twenty years earlier.

AFTER DORIS'S DEATH

Being in such a numb state of shock after Doris' death, the thought of taking another partner was furthest from my mind. On a trip overseas in October 2010 with Rotaplast to Vietnam, I was doing ward rounds in the children's ward and met a paediatrician, Dr. Anne Weurslin, from Colorado Springs U.S.A.

In the course of conversation, I mentioned that my wife had died some nine months ago.

"My husband died a year ago," she said.

We had something in common and started a close friendship. She had been a swimming coach and we went off to swim at resort pools whenever we could. We went wining and dining together frequently. She called me her new "boyfriend" and wrote home about me.

She had inherited a large sum of money from her late husband's estate. People said I was too old for her. She made several advances to me but I didn't take her up. I hadn't had sex for over a year and felt inadequate.

Time came for us to part at the end of the mission.

I said, "You know there are two things amiss in our relationship. One, you live in America and I live in Australia so one of us would have to move and two, you are twenty three years younger than me, which could be a problem later in life."

She agreed, "Let's call it off and perhaps visit later on."

She was a very attractive lady, good looking, educated and intelligent and she sparked the thought in me that perhaps I was not too old to look for and find another partner.

MY SEARCH FOR COMPANIONSHIP

I contacted E-Harmony on-line, having seen their advertisements on television. I found their website most user-unfriendly. You are provided with a host of "single" women with very few details unless you paid up more money. You didn't know whether they were widowed, divorced once or multiple times, or never married. You could send a message but only ones provided by them, not your own. I signed off after a month, most unimpressed.

I made the decision to go on a cruise over Christmas when my medico-legal practice was on holiday. I booked a cruise to New Zealand with Scenic Cruises. At the first dinner I met a German/Australian person named Franz and told him I would like to meet someone. He likewise was looking for female companionship after a three month separation from his wife whom he told me had a severe mental disorder making her impossible to live with. He told me he had watched all the arrivals at the ship's gangplank and had spied out a group of four single women and had arranged to meet them for dinner. I joined them at dinner. They were all dancing friends and had booked the cruise together. Franz had picked out a pretty Dutch lady (Mien) for himself and I found a good looking English lady named Rozanne. She was as tall as me at five feet ten and a half inches. We formed an instant friendship and went on excursions from the boat to inland New Zealand together. We wined and dined and had a lovely time.

After the cruise, on the days I came to Sydney when working in my medico-legal practice, I visited Rozanne in her home at French's Forest.

After about a month together, Rozanne told me she couldn't accept my bad manners (not opening doors for her), my hearing loss and my chronic cough. I suggested we give our friendship more time to sort out. Wrong decision!

Rozanne from then on was hypercritical of me, so I wrote down all the things she said about me, such as I was developing 'old-timer's' dementia and had an "Australian attitude to women", etc., etc. I stopped recording these comments after the list reached thirty.

Rozanne was a pensioner and earned some extra money teaching dancing. I took up Latin Ballroom dancing and joined a Newcastle group under Zara. I learned cha cha, rhumba, quickstep, foxtrot, samba, waltz, tango, everything.

My relationship with Rozanne slowly faded. She ran a ballroom dance on her birthday (born 12th May 1939) in 2011. We parted company. She asked me to tell her what was wrong with her. I did and gave her a copy of the comments she had made about me. In return she wrote a rather vitriolic, sarcastic email. I was not surprised with her reaction, as I knew she had difficulty handling any criticism.

In July 2012 I went to Ricionne in Italy, swimming with FINA World Championships Masters. I was at a loose end and during the trip I met a masters swimmer from Warringah Club in Sydney. Her name was Joy. She was accompanying a friend who had Alzheimer 's disease. Joy had been a widow for about a year and a half and was quite well off financially. She had a delightful personality and ever-smiling face. We frequently dined and toured together when not swimming. Unfortunately I could not get her alone to try chatting her up because of her job as carer for her demented friend.

After FINA and back in Australia, I met up with Joy and we continued wining and dining together. She was an amateur filmmaker and told me she had a Jewish friend 'Ami' who was in the same field. He was ten years younger than her and I was ten years older. He worked as an IT consultant. Joy's family told her I was too old for her. Following several nice trips to Alice Springs Masters Games and PAN-PAC Masters Games on the Gold Coast, she announced she would be going with 'Ami' and so our friendship ended.

I went on-line with R.S.V.P. (Respondez s'il vous plaît), an Australian dating website. It was much more user-friendly in that you were able to write out your own story and what you would like in a friend. You had to put your date of birth and a recent photo or two. I had many meetings with contacts. The first lady I met lived in Kincumber on the Central Coast and as I was going swimming at Woy Woy I met her at the pool. On meeting her, I could see that she did not match up with her photo which was taken at least ten years earlier and she was significantly heavier than she appeared in her photo. Dishonesty is not a good start to a relationship so I did not meet her again.

I met many women and had at least twelve contacts over coffee in a convenient restaurant. Most were not suitable. One lady's photo looked good at a distance. When I met her she told me she weighed 120kgs but at six feet two inches could carry the weight. I don't feel comfortable with obese women so we did not meet again.

Another lady was a dentist. Like me, she did overseas charity work in her holidays, in her case, in Hungary. We met in a restaurant in Lane Cove in Sydney. It was a Take-Away Pizza place with a few tables. I could not think of a worse place to meet anyone. I asked her if she had any health problems.

"Yes, I have an auto-immune deficiency and have to go into hospital every three months for a week's I.V. antibiotic therapy to prevent a severe, possibly fatal infection."

"Oh, no," I thought.

On RSVP I saw an entry from a lady named Val who lived in Newcastle 10 minutes' drive away. Val was one year older than me and had been a nurse. Her main sport was golf. Our first meeting was over coffee and when I went to greet her with a hug and a kiss, she shied away. She had been divorced from her alcoholic husband after her four children had grown up and later married an old school friend who was related to the Steggles chicken farming family. He was three years older and sadly developed prostate cancer dying a few years before I met her.

Val and I had a lot in common. We played golf at the Newcastle Golf Club course. We went to classical music recitals and dined out often. She lived in a two-storied semi-detached flat with two bedrooms upstairs. On my first visit there she told me bluntly, "There are two bedrooms upstairs and you are not seeing them." No chance of intimacy there!

Her daughters were nurses, her grandsons were long distance swimming champions and there was an anaesthetist doctor in-law. She occasionally came swimming with me in the summer. She was of a slim build and five foot three inches tall. She had a pleasant, weathered face with a nice agreeable personality. She also walked quite quickly for her age.

Our platonic friendship continued with just a handshake and no other contact.

After about a year, I asked her if she had any feelings for me.

"There is no chemistry," I said. Thereafter, I signed our emails as N.C.B. (No chemistry Bill).

I reckoned Val had had two difficult relationships, which had left her emotionally traumatised and she wasn't willing to commit to a third relationship. We kept in touch by email and after a few years, we met for a meal near her home. I showed her a photo of me with Angela. I told Val I had another interest and we parted. She was obviously saddened as she had not met up with any other male golfing friend and maybe felt she had missed out.

I had had little success with RSVP and so put an advertisement in the "Seniors" magazine. This comes out monthly and has about twenty t twenty –five women seeking men and about fifteen to twenty men seeking women. I received many replies.

ANGELA

One woman in particular caught my attention. She was a retired associate professor of Geology, Mineralogy and Soil Research.

I met Dr. Angela Jones on 30th November 2012 on a visit to Sydney whilst doing some medico legal work. She confessed that she was one and a half years older than I was but she looked more like seventy than eighty-five years. 'You are going to live a long life' I said to myself. No health problems, fit and active, likes swimming and could play golf. Perfect!

Angela was born in Scotland in 1927 and was educated at Aberdeen University. She came to Australia for a job at Melbourne University and there met her husband Lloyd. He was a smoker and had died some fourteen years before we met.

Angela and I hit it off very well. We went to concerts, shows, swimming, golf and everything together. Travelling from Newcastle down to Sydney for work, I began to stay overnight with Angela. She lived in a small house in Mosman - too small to fit me in, with no garage and three flights of stairs. I suggested she needed a step-free house for her old age and one with two garages for each of our cars. She bought a property to fit this description and made me an offer I couldn't refuse. I moved in with her on Australia Day 26th January 2016.

The unit where we live in Mosman is situated conveniently close to shops and the RSL Club as well has plenty of coffee shops and restaurants within walking distance. It is also close to the Mosman Bowling Club, which I joined soon after meeting Angela.

We drive about two and a half kilometres to Balmoral Beach to swim in the ocean baths. When the water gets too cold I move to the heated six-lane 25 metre pool at Spit Junction, about one kilometre away. We go to Terry Hills for golf practice and also to play an 18 hole par 3 course. It is short and not too much walking for us oldies.

Angela and Bill, 2014

I share all living expenses with Angela including electricity, gas, water and food. Angela doesn't charge me rent. Since my illness in January 2018 I have stopped work entirely and my only income is from a unit I bought in Charlestown, Newcastle, and a few shares. I spend more than I make (who doesn't?) and am drawing money from my piggy bank (managed funds). I expect that to run out in about four years if I am still around. I can then sell my unit and spend that until I die!

CHATSWOOD CHRISTADELPHIAN ECCLESIA

I had been visiting Angela in her house for three years from November 2012 staying the odd overnight when I had work in Sydney on two consecutive days. In 2016, I moved to be with her in Mosman and have attended Chatswood Christadelphian Church on Sundays. As they have only about twelve regular members and no paid ministry, I was a welcome addition to share the load of ecclesiastical duties. These include the "exhortation" (the sermon), the chairmanship, reading the Bible passages, giving the ecclesial prayer, giving prayers for the sacraments, bread and wine, the closing prayer and singing hymns.

As most of the members had given the sermon many times, I was a welcome fresh exhorter. I had been exhorting about every six months in Charlestown Church and had kept my talks, all fully written out, for twenty-six years. Therefore, I was able to update them and recycle my talks. They liked and enjoyed my approach to Christianity and as a non-Christadelphian hereditary church member, I had a different approach to my 'sermons'.

Chatswood also imports speakers from Christadelphian churches all around Sydney, but mainly from Shaftsbury Road, Burwood, Ryde, Hurstville, and Wollongong.

The fact that I am living with Angela in a de facto relationship and not married posed a problem for the church but my contribution to church duties is too great to be cancelled so my non-married situation has been overlooked.

Angela is a lapsed Anglican who gave up religion in her university years and considers herself an atheist. I have been in the same situation so can relate to that. I have explained to her my views and would say that she is more agnostic now than atheist. We agree to disagree on the subject but she probably knows more about the Christadelphian religion than many non-Christadelphians and I believe I am having a long-term effect on her rejection of Christ.

It took me twenty-three years of living with my Christadelphian wife, Doris, before I searched for the "truth" of the meaning of the Bible and in reading the New Testament with an open mind I found the meaning of Christ's message: the "pearl of great price" which we have. I pray for Angela to find that pearl.

A friend once said to me that he knew many intelligent people who were practising Christians.

"There must be something in it, otherwise millions wouldn't follow it!"

How right he was.

11 MY SEPTIC ARTHRITIS
- THE WORST ILLNESS OF MY LIFE

After our successful cruise with Holland America on the *Nordam*, we unpacked on Friday 5th January 2018 and I spent some time answering mail and the more important items on the internet. Angela had a bout of diarrhoea in the last two days of the trip but recovered on arrival in Australia.

On Saturday the sixth, I went for my usual morning swim of about eight hundred metres at Balmoral Baths. After breakfast, I developed a severe fever with rigors and shivering. Angela put me out in the sun where I promptly vomited in the garden. Bouts of vomiting followed by for the next four to six hours with resting in bed in between. I was dizzy and febrile. I expected to recover in a day or so as I usually did. It was not to be.

I spent a miserable Sunday taking Panadol and resting in bed. I slept in the spare room so as not to disturb Angela. About midnight I woke to go to the toilet and on getting out of bed fell flat on my face due to dizziness. I cut myself in several places on my face and couldn't get back into bed. I tried crawling to get to Angela but she had her hearing aids out and couldn't hear my cries for help. After two hours of very slow progress, I decided to wait until morning when Angela found me.

We summoned the ambulance and I was taken to Royal North Shore Hospital Emergency Department where I was admitted to ICU for three days. I had about fifteen to twenty drips and wires going everywhere. I had developed septicaemia with septic arthritis of the left knee joint - a rare but severe complication of gastroenteritis.

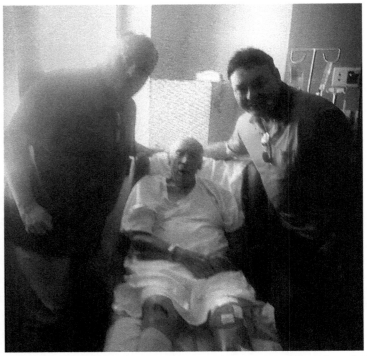

In hospital with septicaemia and septic arthritis of the left knee. Sons Colin and David visiting

My left knee was aspirated and drew a virulent fluid, which had strep pyogenes in it, sensitive to penicillin. I was put on intra venous antibiotics for the next six and a half weeks. I developed a deep vein thrombosis and my left leg swelled to about twice its normal size.

I was dehydrated and given IV fluid (too little at 800 mls in six hours) and developed auricular fibrillation with heart failure which fortunately responded to treatment. I lost nearly half my red blood cells (HB from 14 to 8) and received two blood transfusions.

I had my left knee washed out by Dr Andrew Ellis. The extremely severe pain prevented me from standing, sitting or rolling over in bed. I was catheterised for two and a half weeks.

I was put on oral antibiotics which soon gave me antibiotic diarrhoea with the embarrassment of dirtying my nappy regularly. I thought of counteracting this with Immodium or Gastrostop which, when ordered, immediately cured the problem.

Finally after nearly seven weeks in RNSH, I was transferred to the Greenwich Rehab Unit - a much nicer hospital. The food was so much better. I had developed anorexia due to not eating the poor food at RNSH and lost thirteen kilograms becoming skin and bone by the time I left.

Rehab consisted of physio twice a day, Monday to Friday but closed on weekends when you are on your own. The physiotherapists pushed hard to get maximum performance and I improved steadily. I could only do three push-ups from the chair at the start but could soon do twenty. The swelling in my knee settled slowly from week to week. After five and a half weeks, the doctor considered me fit enough to return home with Angela monitoring.

I used a walking frame, a walking stick and car to get around to shops and the swimming pool. I did exercises on the back patio. The rehab hospital staff told me I would get ongoing physio as an outpatient but there was no sign of that. I went swimming but, due to a lack of buoyancy and leg movement, I sank and could hardly swim at half pace.

The long-term future was, at that stage, undecided. However, my knee sepsis finally settled allowing me to get back to normal after several months.

12 MY SPORTS

SWIMMING

Without ever having a swimming lesson, I won my age races at school and represented Sydney University in breaststroke. I came second each year to the Australian champion.

We had trips away to Perth, Brisbane and Melbourne. It was most enjoyable.

My swimming was put on hold in my early years of medical practice except for one match in 1957 with the Children's Hospital in Perth. The Medical Superintendent, Dr. Godfrey, who was an excellent fast freestyle swimmer, organised a relay meeting each year based on doctors at hospitals. Our team, including me, won in that year, 1957.

For exercise, I used to swim about six hundred metres up to one kilometre a day when I came back to Newcastle in 1968. One of my friends was involved in Masters swimming and asked me to join in. I also did "fun runs" of five or ten kilometres until I tore a ligament (tibialis posterior) in my ankle which stopped me jogging.

I decided to do more swimming and contacted the Novacastrian Swimming Club in September 1999. I entered my first race in Woy Woy and won it. The adrenalin buzz from competition set me going and I entered most Masters swimming events. Together with these came our club training nights and I had my first swimming lesson at seventy. I had many private lessons and apart from stroke correction, the most important thing I learned was how to train to improve one's speed. I won medals at state and national level, mainly in breaststroke, butterfly and individual medley.

My first overseas trip was to Christchurch, New Zealand in 2002. I won 7th and 8th medals in 100 and 200 metre breaststroke. I recall lining up in the 70 to 74 age group race with four of the participants having nominated swimming times faster than the Australian record! The competition was severe and a higher level than I had encountered before.

Swimming Butterfly at Canberra Masters Games 2003

I went in the FINA World Masters Swimming every two years and also some World Masters games in which the swimming events were not as competitive as the FINA swimming, having only one third to half as many swimmers.

SWIMMING CHAMP PROVES HE'S NEVER TOO OLD FOR GOLD

Caroline Tang

MOSMAN resident Bill Walker, OAM, turns 88 on Sunday but he's already thinking about hitting 90 and competing in the 2019 FINA World Masters Championships.

The retired plastic surgeon, former overseas aid surgeon and Mosman Rotarian only had his first formal swimming lesson at age 70. "At age 7 years, with the help of my older sisters, I learned dog paddle in Clovelly ocean baths and learned breaststroke and freestyle by watching others," Dr Walker said. "We had to walk one mile to and from the baths because we were too poor to pay the one penny fare."

He swam competitively in school and university and started masters events when he turned 70.

Dr Walker holds 20 international gold medals and won four gold in the World Masters Games last month, despite a broken rib before his last race. "I have been described as a competitive animal. I swim better if I've got to beat somebody," he said.

Dr Walker moved to Mosman last year. "People ask why I came to live here and the answer is very simple: a woman," he said.

Mosman Daily, 11ᵗʰ May 2017

Retired plastic surgeon Bill Walker is a swimming champion at age 87. Picture: Annika Enderborg

Across the Lake (Lake Macquarie) Swim, 3.8
kilometres. My sixth in 2010

I was co-opted to swim in world relays by other
world champions. These were George Corones
(from Queensland), Patrick Galvin (Marlin
Masters, Victoria), Tony Goodwin (World
Champion in breaststroke from Sydney) and John
Cox (also Marlin Masters). We won two gold
medals for the four by fifty metres freestyle for
the combined 320 years age group, and the four
by fifty medley at Gotenburg, Sweden, 2012, and
Montreal, Canada when we broke the 320 years
four by fifty medley record.

I also enjoyed great success at the PAN-PAC
Masters Games in Southport, Queensland winning
lots of gold medals.

I was voted Masters Male Swimmer of the Year,
2004 and I repeated that effort in 2014 with the
same award and again broke eleven national

records and twelve state records. I repeated this achievement yet again in 2019 and I was voted NSW Masters swimmer of the year. Because of Covid, the presentation was delayed until February 2021.

My best overseas meeting was at Kazan, Russia, in 2015. I won five gold medals out of five races. This may have been due to a poor roll-up of entries with only about a third of the number for the FINA World Swimming that year.

I had a whole year off with illness in 2018 but returned to training for the Worlds in South Korea in 2019 in the 90 to 94 age group.

FINA World Swimming Championships, Gwanju, South Korea, 2019. Four Gold and One Silver

The championships were held at Gwanju. I won four gold medals: 50m butterfly, 200m individual medley, 100 and 200m breaststroke. I also won a silver medal in 200m backstroke.

HOCKEY

I took up hockey at high school in preference to rugby league football, which my parents said was too dangerous a game. (I agree with them now). Swimming was my summer sport in preference to cricket. Representing Sydney University in hockey, I played in first grade and intervarsity in the left wing position, having a good back stick.

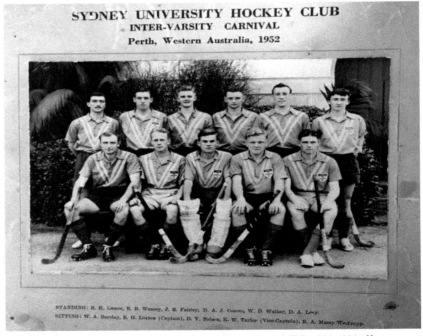

Sydney University Hockey Team 1952. W. Walker
back row second from right

Later, in Newcastle, I played hockey again and in the western suburbs, playing in third grade and 'Police Boys' third and fourth grades. A fourth grade side, which I coached, won a championship victory.

GOLF

By the time I reached forty-nine, my leg injuries were becoming too common. Torn tendons and a back injury (early disc) led me to give up hockey and switch to golf.

I joined Newcastle Golf Club in January 1978. It had a reputation as the toughest course in the district and lived up to it. You could lose a ball in the rough off every tee and every second shot, which, of course, I did. I regularly lost six balls for each eighteen holes and bought second hand balls at twenty cents each. Paul Robinson of Belmont Golf Club gave me lessons but it took one and a half years before I moved off the maximum handicap of 27. I finally achieved an A Grade handicap of 12 after improving over the years. Newcastle was considered to be three strokes harder than any other course in the district. I taught my two sons and their children how to play.

The tenth hole at Newcastle needed a long drive of 230 to 240 metres to get over a hill onto the flat. I could still do this at age seventy-three and over the years won several long drive competitions and many trophies. As age wore on, my handicap inevitably increased. In 2009, after moving to Greenleaf Retirement Village, I joined Belmont Golf Club with a handicap of 16.

In 2013, Angela and I added lawn bowls to our repertoire.

RACING AND GAMBLING

My father was a bookmaker and told us a number of rules to abide by, such as *never* bet on something unless you have a shade of odds in your favour. He also said there is no such thing as a bet after the race has been won and other maxims. As a result of this, none of us except June became gambling addicts.

There is always someone trying to illegally beat the odds by fair or foul means. I bought a one sixth share in a racehorse in Cessnock, a provincial town near Newcastle The horse was trained by a good trainer and ridden by a top Jockey, Robert Thompson, the trainer's son.

In the saddling paddock before the race, Robert's father would ask him, "Have you heard anything in there?" meaning, is the race fixed for a particular horse to win?

My sister, June, knew a horse breaker/trainer who worked at Randwick Racetrack, named Stewart. She told me Stewart knew all the jockeys and trainers and would wait on the track at the 800 m mark as the horses would go past on to the starting post. "Good day Stewart", they would say then, "Number 5, Stewart."

He had a key to a side door, would race down to the nearby TAB, put a large bet on No. 5 and it always won!

I went to Port Macquarie to play golf with a friend of mine, Warren H. We met at the local racetrack on a Saturday afternoon accompanied by my wife and our two boys in their teens. They had never been to a racetrack before.

At the entrance, the turnstile clerk said, "Get your late ticket after 3pm and you can get in for half price." I paid the fee.

"No ticket! Just see that man up there and he will let you in."

Obviously, they had a deal going on and were sharing the late fees.

I bought a race book and went to the pre-race inspection ring.

I said to the boys, "You pick a horse that looks slim and fit with strong legs."

I selected one and went to the bookies ring. My horse was the rank outsider at 33 to 1. I got Doris to put a dollar on it for me, I was too ashamed to put on such a small bet for a possible $34.

"Ticket number 35", said the bookmaker. The clerk put $35 on the ticket. I told Doris that he had made a mistake and given us thirty-four to one "I`ll take it back", she said.

"No need. We'll just tear it up when it loses."

The horse was running last at the first run past the post with one more lap to go, but started to catch up. At the home turn he was 3rd and swept past the rest to win. He was the best-kept secret of the day. I sent Doris to collect her winnings of $35. She, being scrupulously honest, told the bookies' clerk that he'd paid the wrong amount. A hand went into the bag drawing out extra dollars.

"You paid me a dollar too much."

I absolutely laughed my head off as no-one gives anything back on the racetrack. The surprised look on the bookie and clerks' faces was a picture.

I met Warren and we went to the pre-race track to pick another horse. I selected a horse called *Boutonière*, a French word meaning a button sewer. Six to one on B*eaut One* 'ere, I thought this must win with such a corruption of its name and it did. Came the last race and I picked a horse that came third.

Beside me in the stand was a man who cheered on the winner saying, "That one couldn't lose."

I asked, "Why?"

"Cause I followed the jockey's runner and every jockey in the race was on it. We got four to one."

I later met Warren H at Duntree League Golf Club, Orange and with my two sons, Colin and David, we played as a foursome for the next week. Warren and I decided to have a match as we had close handicaps. We were playing for one ball a hole. Warren indulged in gamesmanship. Just as I was about to putt, he would say in a loud voice, "You've got that for a win or half." He aimed at distracting my concentration. I learnt to counteract this.

"Warren, I know what the score is, now shut up while I putt." I would then concentrate and as often as not sink the putt.

He soon learnt to stop this but would often say when he hit a good drive or chip, "Bet you can't get one past that."

I learnt to overcome this annoyance. I would hit a top drive and you know when you have done so.

I would say to Warren, "Bet you a ball you can't get one past that."

He didn't and after I had won about five balls in this way he realised I was betting *after the race had been won.*

Warren was a golf cheat and I said to my sons after about three days' play, "What is unusual about Warrens play? He has never lost a ball and we all have lost plenty."

They agreed. The way you do this is to carry an identical ball in your pocket and drop it when no one's looking so as to find the lost ball. I made a rule that whenever Warren lost a ball one of us would stay with him during his search until the five-minute time ran out and not surprisingly, he started losing balls.

At the end of the week Warren said, "How many balls am I behind?" It was ten. "I`ll bet you ten balls on the last hole," he said.

"Right, you're on." I won the hole and twenty balls!

In my student days, I would take my mother out to Wentworth Park and Harold Park Dog races in Sydney on a Saturday night. I would bet in small amounts, two shillings up to a maximum of ten shillings a bet. I never won much but never lost much. When on holidays I would sometimes go to a dog race meeting if there was one nearby.

We were at Southport on the Gold Coast with my nephew, Bill Falconer, and we went to the dogs on the Saturday night. We were losing and Bill noted an old lady putting a $200 bet on a dog. This was a large bet for an elderly person. He followed her into the stand and sat beside her. and asked her "What dog do you like in the next race?"

She was an owner trainer and knew her dogs.

She said, "If you want a sure winner, back *Cindy* in the last race."

It was a seven to four favorite, so we put on enough money to get square plus a bit over. It was a long distance race over 700+ metres. When the dogs came out there was Cindy, a tiny bitch weighing almost half the weight of the larger male dogs Off they ran with Cindy staying last to the first turn, and then she sped through the most narrow gap you had ever seen on the rails. She did the same at each turn and at the home turn sped off to win by several lengths down the straight. It pays to be in the know.

BOWLS

I had always been interested in playing bowls and decided at age eighty-three it was a good time to start before it was too late. Because many Saturdays are taken up with swimming competitions we have played only social bowls and I have reached a middle of the road standard.

TENNIS

Over the years, I have enjoyed playing social tennis. Lessons followed in my sixties to improve my game and playing doubles with my sons has now virtually ceased since my serious illness with septicaemia in January 2018.

SAILBOARDING

A patient of mine was getting married and she presented with a thick black mole high on her left back shoulder, which was visible in her wedding dress. She wanted it removed which I duly did.

"Who are you marrying, Isobel?" I asked.

It's John X. You may have heard of him. He recently won the World Sailboarding Championship and has now set up shop in Newcastle."

I had been thinking of learning to sailboard after trying one out on the Gold Coast at a plastic surgeons' meeting.

"Would he have one for sale for a beginner like me?" I inquired.

"I don't know but will ask him."

Two weeks later, I had bought a large heavy sailboard for a very low cost. It came with a single lesson, which taught me how to put it together and the basic rules of sailing it on Lake Macquarie.

Days later, David and I went down to Lake Macquarie to give it a try. I found I could only sail downwind in short bursts before falling off but couldn't sail upwind. As a result we sailed across a section of the lake and drove the car around to where we landed and reloaded it onto my 4WD Toyota.

I persevered with it and my wife recalled me practising at Charlie Brown's place on the lake where I fell off and restarted thirty times! I eventually became reasonably proficient.

At Tanilba Bay, I practised sailboarding with a friend, Jim Wylie. I progressed to a lighter faster French board and in the Bicentennial Year, 1988, I sailed across Lake Macquarie and back twice to prove to myself I could do it.

It was difficult to sail in heavy, windy conditions with choppy water so you didn't go. The younger more expert fellows would go out, but with a short board, and sail it faster with more manoeuvrability. These boards were called *sinkers,* because the board would sink if you stood up on it when stationary with no wind. You had to do a "water-start" which meant getting in the water alongside the board, positioning the sail into the strong wind then allowing the wind to lift you up out of the water with your feet on the side of the board and away you would go. It required quite a degree of expertise and skill and one had to learn.

A friend of mine, Dr Brendan Pell (an anaesthetist), took an eight-day course in sailboarding in Hawaii just to learn how to water start.

One day at Tanilba Bay, I looked at the wind and the choppy water and decided it was too fast and heavy. A young man with a *sinker* was there.

I asked him, "Is the wind fast enough?"

"Not quite," he said.

I realised I still had a long way to go in my sailboard learning.

I gave up sailboarding and passed my board on to Shaun Walker, my grandson. I gave him a lesson on how to sail it but had lost my skills and Shaun never took the trouble to learn how to sail it.

LIGHT AIRCRAFT FLYING

My son, David, wanted to be a pilot so we put him through the pilot training school "NASA" at Cessnock, N.S.W. He passed his Grade 1 Commercial Licence and Pilot Teaching Licence after which he needed pupils.

"Dad, why don't you take up flying?"

I became David's first pupil starting flying at Cessnock at sixty-three. After a few weeks, he moved up to Queensland leaving me with no teacher. My training continued under another teacher at Warnervale on the Central Coast. After about 150 hours of flight training, I received my pilot's licence. Next was an undercarriage rating, a night rating and with 40+ hours into an instrument rating we had a disaster.

I bought a Cessna 210, which is a strong single-engine turbo charged aircraft able to fly at an altitude above 10,000 feet.

My Cessna 210, Mr. H.

We had an undercarriage failure, which, with a damaged propeller, requires the engine to be taken out and checked.

At this time, there was a problem with Mobil fuel. Mobil had put an additive into their aviation fuel to enhance performance. This caused a sludge build-up in the carburettor resulting in fuel stoppage. It was only after three planes needed to do emergency glide-in landings that we discovered the problem.

All planes using Mobil fuel had to have their carburettors checked, including mine. This caused a delay of three months before I could fly again. Mobil would pay for the repair but not for the time lost in use of the aircraft. I did little flying after this and sold "Mr. H", my 210, after five years of flying.

We had a number of memorable flights in "Mr. H", the most notable of which was a flight to Darwin and back with David, Doris and me. We visited remote places like Fitzroy Crossing, Uluru and the Lava Tubes in Queensland. It's a great way to see Australia in a short time.

Light aircraft flying is hazardous and planes crash due to loss of vision in cloud and consequent loss of control resulting in a spiral dive to earth. I did a course in emergency recovery with an aerobatic pilot in a *Pitts Special,* which is a purpose built aerobatic aircraft. My teacher showed me how to do a "wingover", an emergency about turn and a spiral recovery. It was the most exciting thing I ever did in my life. The pilot took me up to 3000 feet and put the plane into a spiral dive heading straight for earth. After three 360 degree rotations, he said, "You can pull it out of the dive now." At about 1500 feet that was very exciting!

With my surgical colleague, John Smyth, we went for a trip around Australia, flying to Dunk Island near the Barrier Reef, Cairns and Darwin. John organised a second trip to Papua New Guinea. I could not go due to work commitments. John with an anaesthetist, three children and one other adult (making six on board the aircraft) set off. I told my son David that John Smyth was going to P.N.G.

David said, "He's a gung ho (risk taking) pilot and will kill himself one day. Do you remember when we went to the Singleton horse sales in his plane? He flew non-visual in cloud for two or three minutes breaking the rules. That's a no-no."

Sure enough, they were in Port Moresby wanting to cross the hazardous central mountain range to Lae. It's a zig-zag course through these mountains which are 18,000 feet on each side. Visual cues of where to turn are difficult to pick. A commercial pilot told me that new commercial pilots are monitored through seven crossings before being allowed to fly solo through. John was running late in Port Moresby and was told by three aircraft personnel, "Don't go, you will be caught in cloud." John went ahead and all six died in the crash. His wife at home had a dream about where he crashed and rang the authorities. Sure enough, that's where they were found.

P.N.G. is said to be "The Graveyard of Pilots" and certainly lived up to its name on this occasion. It was lucky I didn't go but perhaps I could have talked John out of flying that day.

ICING UP

If you fly in cold cloudy conditions in small aircraft, there is the risk of icing up. Ice accumulates on the wings making them heavier and less efficient causing the plane to go down. It's possible for the ice to melt off at a lower flight level.

We flew around Alaska and a pilot told me that it is almost impossible to fly in cloud on instruments because of the risk of icing up. One very experienced lady pilot decided to fly to Anchorage over some high mountains or along a narrow valley pass. She iced up and descended rapidly, still in cloud, but fortunately, by skilful use of her G.P.S., she navigated through the valley pass de-icing at 1000 feet. It was a lucky escape.

At the time I was flying, a group of four, including several doctors, were flying from Wollongong to Canberra on a Sunday evening. The pilot in charge, who had many hours of flying experience, decided to go over the mountains on instruments to get to Canberra in time for work commitments next day. The wings iced up causing the plane to crash into the mountains and killing everyone aboard.

A meteorologist told me after examining the meteorological report that they were one hundred percent certain to have iced up. They were trying to make a deadline. There is always another day. In my five years of flying, on three or four occasions I made the decision not to fly, which was the right one every time!

13 MORE ON MY SPORTING AND OTHER ACTIVITIES

RIFLE SHOOTING

At the age of nine, in Sofala near Bathurst NSW, my brother Ted took me out shooting rabbits. With Ted's instruction, I shot my first rabbit. It was exciting. I went rabbit shooting in Cessnock and in Cooma where my sister Olive lived. I found spotlight shooting at night a successful pursuit, too.

Shortly after arriving in Tara, Queensland, in my first solo practice, I was invited to join the rifle club. At the club, people shot big bore rifles over 300, 500, 800 and 900 metres. Using peep sights, I had to judge wind and adjust sights to allow for drift.

A book by an ophthalmologist named Dr Sweet helped me with the best technique in rifle shooting needed to get the best result. Consequently, I became an "A" Grade shooter within a year and as well as a good coach.

I represented Darling Downs District at Belmont Rifle Club shooting for the Murray Shield, ten shooters firing fifteen counting shots at 600 metres. I came third in our team and we won the Murray Shield against fifteen other teams.

Originally we used World War One rifles, .303 calibre Short Magazine Lee Enfields, but these were replaced by NATO FN 762 rifles which were much more accurate. As a result, they had to change the bullseye on targets to include an inner circle about half the size of the original bullseye. This counted for an extra 0.1 points but sorted out the shooters, as many could shoot 10/10 on the original centre bullseye. We separated the drawn scores on a one on one shootout, a knockout competition.

I took up rifle shooting in Scotland shortly after arriving and came second in the "Scottish National" shoot. As an Australian, I could not shoot for Scotland even though with a name like Willy Walker I could have passed myself off as a Scotsman with grandparent heritage.

When I moved to Wythenshawe, Manchester, I joined the local rifle club there and enjoyed some success with a top score of the day at an interclub shoot against a top English club.

BISLEY

The mecca of all big bore rifle shooting is the Bisley Rifle Range in Woking, Surrey, just outside London. Each year in July, over 1000 shooters meet to compete in long-range rifle shooting. This has been a military exercise since before World War I and the trophy room is filled with large and small cups.

The main competition is held over 300 metres, followed by a knockout for 300 shooters at 600 metres and, finally, a hundred shooters at 900 metres. I never got past the Stage II six hundred metres but won a cup in an "extra" competition for those who didn't make it to the end. I won at 600 metres with my fifteen shots scoring fourteen bullseyes and one inner, so I can claim to have my name on a trophy at Bisley.

On return to Australia, I continued rifle shooting in Newcastle maintaining the position as second best shooter in the club.

I took up pistol shooting a few years later and achieved "A" Grade level in Standard Pistol and Air pistol, with "B" Grade in the others. I gave up pistol shooting in the early 1970s after about five years with the club.

WILLY ON STAGE

I played in a male ballet to the music of Swan Lake. As the lead "prima donna", I had to attempt difficult steps, which resulted in my falling over and rolling on the ground. Again, there was much laughter from the audience.

In the course of my medical career, I have been involved in slapstick comedy in the form of hospital "reviews" performed by medical staff, mostly at Royal Newcastle Hospital.

Ballet Dancer Bill, leaving the stage

In the opening scene of a skit about an operation, which I wrote, the patient was on the operating table with theatre sister, anaesthetist and assistant surgeon present. My scalpel is held high in the air like a dagger and, I plunge it into the patient's abdomen who nearly jumps off the bed.

"Can't you get her to sleep," I shout to the anaesthetist who promptly produces a large soft hammer and hits her on the head. With the abdomen open, I pull out intestines (sausages), a kidney, a liver and then I find a watch.

"I wondered where I lost that watch," I say, then to the anaesthetist (named Owen James or "O.J", the hospital's chief anaesthetist), "Is she OK OJ?"

He replies, "Yes, but I am a bit worried about her Hb, CRP, SGOT and particularly her N.I.B. (health insurance fund)."

The patient starts waking up.

"OJ, can't you get her to sleep - any stage of anaesthesia between death and movement will do."

"Isn't it better that she moves than dies?" says OJ.

"You've got me by the short and curlies there," says I. The audience were really getting into it and enjoying themselves.

Eventually I find a fountain pen in the wound and close with the words, "The pen is mightier than the scalpel."

In another skit on another occasion, I was the patient in bed with no lines and nothing to do. I wasn't prepared for this so I asked what is wrong with the patient? They said he has hematemesis (vomiting of blood).

"Just give me two minutes before the consulting staff arrives, okay?"

In bed, I sit up and cock my ear to the sounds of approaching staff. I quickly take a bottle of tomato sauce from my locker and take a swig, spitting it out onto a towel at the bedside. I then collapse back into an agonising pose awaiting the doctors. My act brought on much laughter from the audience.

We presented a number of these skits along with many others over the years, but sadly in today's busy generation the "hospital review" seems to have disappeared.

After I had resumed music lessons, I was invited by an anaesthetic registrar to join a "jug" band playing cello base, with him playing the guitar, another played a washboard tympani, a fourth person blew over bottle tops for woodwind effect, and another played drums. Our band played blues and old-time jazz.

For one solo cello item, I set myself on a seat centre stage, playing "Baa Baa Black Sheep" starting a mid-cello and repeating an octave higher each time. I instructed the curtain attendant to bring down the curtain when I had played the third tune. When the fourth time came and the curtain didn't come down, I played the tune for the fifth time, high up on the "A" string and was running out of a string to play any higher. The attendant woke up to his job and let the curtain down with some speed. It hit me on my head very nearly knocking me off my perch. It caused much laughter from the audience who thought it part of the act.

MY MUSICAL CAREER

My mother always had two pianos in the house so that two people could practise at one time. All the girls were taught piano but not the boys.

At the age of twelve, my mother noticed I could play tunes on the piano without any lessons.

"Perhaps we had better have you taught," she said.

Olive and I were taught piano at the local convent school, I believe St. Bernards. Our teacher was Sister Augusta. We both sat and passed grade six piano with a credit - an amazing result. I used to practise two hours a day without being asked to do so. We noticed that our teacher had a chronic cough and shortly after our exam, she died of tuberculosis.

A substitute teacher (of violin) was next to useless and my mother said, "As you're sitting the leaving certificate exam the next year, you should stop piano lessons."

During my second year studying Medicine at Sydney University, I decided to take some piano lessons at the conservatorium under a Ms. Blanche. I found it too difficult to practise and study at the same time so stopped lessons after one year.

In the UK, I decided to have Alison and Colin taught the violin in Manchester under a student teacher (Jamie). In helping the children, I found I was becoming a second hand violinist so suggested to Jamie that I should learn the cello.

"Too hard for me to teach you." she said, "Why not leave it until you get back to Australia."

PLAYING THE CELLO

In February 1969, after settling into plastic surgery practice, I presented myself to Osric Fife at the Newcastle conservatorium. It was just three months short of my fortieth birthday.

Bill playing the cello

"Why do you want to learn the cello at your age?" said Osric.

To me this was like waving a red flag at a bull. "Who can tell me I can't do it?"

I practised hard and six months later Osric said, "You are doing quite well. My last Dr. pupil lasted only four lessons."

I felt like saying, 'We are not all the same.'

I knew the doctor who only tried the cello on prompting from his wife, an accomplished pianist. He was not musical.

I continued studies with Osric for ten years doing *no* exams. Later, a Sydney cellist, Susan Blake, taught me. She was an excellent teacher who concentrated more on correct technique. She improved my playing tremendously. I sat the seventh grade cello exam and passed. I started on A Mus. A (Associate in Music, Australia) When my teacher left to go overseas on a sabbatical, I had a replacement teacher, Ms. X, but failed A Mus. A. When Susan returned, I re-sat the exam but failed again mainly because I could not put in enough practice with a weekly fifty hours plus surgical practice. I gave the cello a rest and someone gave me a viola. I took lessons for five years but when my teacher left to live in Turkey with her husband running a travel agency, I failed to get a replacement teacher.

I took up piano lessons again and sat grade six with a pass. I sat grade seven and thought i would pass but failed. The Australian Music Examinations Board messed up my exam time so the exam was held in a private dwelling in Newcastle. There was one other seventh grade student in an adjacent room. I could hear her test. I thought she would pass easily but she too failed.

I had a phone call from the teacher whose home we used, to inform me that her seventh grader also failed. She said she had nine pupils of preliminary or first grade piano who all failed, her worst result in fifty years.

There was obviously a severe examiner. I wrote to the AMEB suggesting there should be some quality control and was told they were looking at it and would have a result in five years! I gave up piano.

During my cello playing life, I played in local symphony orchestras for over thirty years. I also joined The Amateur Chamber Music Society of NSW and played in chamber music groups in Sydney and at the annual Wollongong meeting over the January long weekend.

My deafness caused me to stop orchestral playing and the after-effects of my septic arthritis now stops me carrying my cello up and down stairs. I go to Newcastle to play with Dr. Jeanette Abery. She has a group of four to eight musicians who play chamber music once a month. I have been going for about fifteen years.

On my trip to Malawi, I met Michael King, chief surgeon at Blantyre, and his wife Elspeth. She was a university lecturer and played viola. She put together a group of string-playing students for violin, viola and cello. I took a cello on my second visit and played in the group. I gave my one and only ever masterclass in how to play the cello. I left the cello there for some years taking it back when I left.

14 MY AMAZING FRIEND HUNTER J.H.FRY

Hunter John Hall Fry, 1932 - 2018

I first met Hunter Fry in Glasgow in 1966 when I was studying plastic surgery with Dr.s Tough and McGregor and Hunter was with Jake Mustardee at Ayreshire. Jake ran a monthly clinic in Glasgow, which we both attended. Hunter was a few years ahead of me in training and asked me to contact him after I had set up in practice in Newcastle.

In 1971, I spent a week with him in Melbourne and he lined up a list of appointments for me to meet all Victoria's leading plastic surgeons, including the famous Sir Benjamin Rank (Father of Plastic surgery in Australia) John Hueston and several other dignitaries.

Hunter was born in 1931 and died on 17th August 2018 aged eighty-seven. He was educated in Melbourne schools and University and achieved his FRACS (Plastics) in 1965. He was a high achiever and won fellowships to USA and a Hunterian Professorship in the UK. He did some research on rabbits' septal (nose) cartilage showing how it one could bend it by ribbing one side. This is a useful technique for rhinoplasty. He was interested in Repetitive Strain Injury in musicians and dancers, and was a foundation member of the Performing Arts Medical Society and contributed many papers to it. He was an excellent pianist and passed the Licentiate Examinations of the Royal Academy of Music, its highest exam. He could play piano concertos. His son, James, became a clarinet leader of a New Zealand symphony orchestra.

On one of my visits, he had bought two Steinway grand pianos on approval, one full sized concert grand and one a size below it. He used to invite visiting world famous pianists to come and play on his piano. He had them sign their names inside and there was the famous *Vladimir Ashkenazy's* signature.

Hunter was married three times and had five children. He was a perfectionist in his personality, which I guess, made him hard to live with at times. On one of my visits to him in Melbourne he was going to Albury for a weekend with two young children and was running late for the plane at Essendon Airport He drove at breakneck speed just making it through red lights with the comment, "Mostly orange!'

We arrived at the airport and he sent me on to the departure desk with the children. On presentation of the tickets the official grabbed a phone saying, *"Hold that plane*! Quick Mr. Fry, come to the aircraft.'

'I am not Mr. Fry. He's parking the car." Hunter arrived soon after.

"Have you ever missed one?" I asked.

"Yes," said Hunter.

In later years, Hunter worked as a medico-legal consultant with companies *IMO Medlaw* and *Sinergy,* his last job. He worked in Melbourne, Canberra, Sydney and Newcastle five days a week. He was a prodigious worker.

On a visit to my hometown, Newcastle, one night, he had a severe nosebleed. He called me and I saw him in his motel room. He had lost at least 200 ml of blood. He was on Warfarin, a blood thinner for heart disease, having had mitral valve surgery. We put him in John Hunter Hospital where the bleeding was stopped with nasal catheters. He returned to Royal North Shore Private where they could not stop the bleeding without withdrawal of his Warfarin. This caused him to have an embolic clot to the brain resulting in a stroke. He was left with a significant memory loss and became very slow to recall or answer simple questions. At that point he ceased his medico legal practice.

Hunter spent the last twelve years of his life living with a long-term friend, Gwinnie Hawke, whom he described as the love of his life. He had a hip replacement operation and died of complications a few weeks later. I was overseas and missed his funeral.

Hunter was one of my dearest medical friends and he helped me a lot in my profession.

ACKNOWLEDGEMENTS

Thanks to my editor and friend, Bruce Walker, for typing, corrections, suggested omissions and additions in the compilation of this book; also to Jan Mitchell for further editing, formatting and publication of the final draft.

Thanks to my late wife, Doris, for her support and nursing expertise in many of my overseas trips.

Thanks to Lyn Thorpe for her introduction and her practical support in eighteen overseas trips.

Thanks to my medical colleagues, Dr.s Newton, Howe, Sillar and members of the Head and Neck Cancer Clinic, and the Cleft Lip and Palate Clinic, who have worked with me over many years.

The photograph of Hunter Fry is copied from the website of the Australian Society of Plastic Surgeons.

Lastly, thanks to my wife Angela, who has made many useful comments in the preparation of this book.

Bill Walker.
June 2020

ABOUT WILLIAM DOWNING WALKER

Order of Australia Medal, 1999

Born 14th May, 1929 at Randwick, Sydney

MY EDUCATION CV

Educated at Randwick primary and Katoomba High schools LC 1947

MB BS Sydney University, January 1954

Hospital Practise JRMO Cessnock 1954

General practise Cessnock, 1955

SRMO Parramatta Hospital, 1956

RMO Princess Margaret Hospital for Children Perth WA, 1957

Registrar in general surgery Royal Perth Hospital, 1958

RMO Tara District hospital (General Practice),1959-1962

Study UK for part 1 FRCS, 1962

SRMO and Registrar in general surgery, Hairmyres Hospital East Kilbride, 1963-66

FRCS Edinburgh 1965

Registrar in plastic surgery Glasgow Royal Infirmary, 1966-7

Registrar in Plastic Surgery, Wythenshawe Hospital, Manchester, 1967-68

Director of plastic surgery, Hunter Area Health Service, 1968-94

FRACS(Plastic surgery), 1970

Foundation Member of the Australian Society of Aesthetic Plastic Surgeons (A.S.A.P.S.) and Cosmetic Plastic Surgeons.

President, N.S.W. Handclub, 1979

Member, Australian Handclub

Member, A.C.L.A.P.A. (Australian Cleft Lip and Palate Association).

3rd World plastic surgery, 1987-2015.

Private Practice in Plastic surgery, 1968-94

OAM (Order of Australia Medal) 1999 for Third World Plastic Surgery

I have done forty-one trips to developing countries to February 2015

***

MY ROTARY CV

Paul Harris Fellow as a non-Rotarian, 1985, for work on Margaret Ilukol

Second Paul Harris Fellowship, 2009

Joined Hamilton Rotary club, 1991. President 1998

Paul Harris silver bar, 1994

Service above self-award, 2004 (Presented annually to one in 100,000 Rotarians by approval of The Rotary International Board)

Joined Newcastle Sunrise Rotary Club, 2005

Len Avard award for Services to PNG, 2007

District 9670 RAM (Rotarians Against Malaria) Representative for approximately eleven years to circa 2011.

ROMAC (Rotarian Oceana Medical Aid For Children) for six years to 2012

Mosman Rotary club 2013-2018

CPSIA information can be obtained
at www.ICGtesting.com
Printed in the USA
BVHW091314010621
608554BV00008B/1224